ALTAR-EGOS

Resolving Conflict, Confronting
Anger and Dealing with Difficult
People in the Church

ALTAR-EGOS

Resolving Conflict, Confronting
Anger and Dealing with Difficult
People in the Church

Dr. Cal LeMon

Altar-Egos: Resolving Conflict, Confronting Anger and Dealing with Difficult People in the Church
by Dr. Cal LeMon

Copyright © 2018 Dr. Cal LeMon
All rights reserved

Published by HigherLife Development Services, Inc.
PO Box 623307
Oviedo, Florida 32762
(407) 563-4806
www.ahigherlife.com

ISBN 13: 978-0-9994156-6-5
ISBN 10: 0-9994156-6-2

First Edition
14 15 16 17 18 —2 1 12 11 10 9 8 7
Printed in the United States of America

DEDICATION

For the last fifty years of my life, I have savored the comfort, the challenges, the honesty, the truth and the tears/laughter with my best friend and life-companion...Kathy. This gifted woman has pushed me, corrected me and then invited me to dance with her when only the two of us could hear the music. My alter-ego is Kathy LeMon.

TABLE OF CONTENTS

INTRODUCTION

I HAVE COME to an important conclusion in these sunset days of my life. Faith is not for the faint of heart. God called Noah to build the first ocean liner; Moses to lead weak, wobbling, whiners through Death Valley; and the apostle Paul to boldly confront his accusers with these words, *"I am in chains for Christ"* (Phil. 1:13).

Once a Christian enthusiastically states, "Jesus Christ is Lord," this individual also has made a decision to continuously ask this question: "What would Jesus do?" This is a dangerous question.

In the words of Dietrich Bonhoeffer, "When God calls a man, He bids him come and die."[1] For the Christian, this dying is actually living. When we live with, and for, Jesus Christ, we begin to understand our eternity has already begun.

This is the Good News.

The difficult news is the church is a depository of imperfect people who can sing in unison all five verses of "The Church's One Foundation" and then quietly skewer each other later on in the day.

This book addresses this contrast in the church: parishioners love God but often struggle with loving each other.

---

[1] Dietrich Bonhoeffer, *The Cost of Discipleship* (New York: Simon and Shuster, 1995), 11.

In other words, we, the church, often choose to not tell each other the truth.

Each of the ten chapters define a specific reason why a follower of Jesus Christ would choose to avoid telling another believer the truth.

Each chapter also will provide practical suggestions to help you verbally address someone in the body of Christ with whom you may not agree.

The best and worst moments in our lives are when we tell each other the truth. The delivery of the truth determines whether we build bridges or create another emotional crater.

This book will provide biblical principles about how to worship with other believers who do not share your view of God and how to be assertive without becoming aggressive when resolving conflict in the church.

This book, *Altar-Egos: Resolving Conflict, Confronting Anger and Dealing with Difficult People in the Church,* begins and ends at an altar. If Christ is the Lord of our lives, then our alter-egos will be truly altered and His words will echo through our egos.

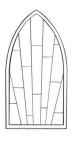

CHAPTER ONE

WE DO NOT TELL THE TRUTH
BECAUSE THE TRUTH CAN HURT

MORALLY, WE HAVE clear categories about what is right or wrong. Is it acceptable to kick the crutches out from someone who recently broke his leg? Is it morally right to intentionally cheat on an IRS return? Is it ethically appropriate to fake a phantom health emergency, so an employee can call in sick to keep a fishing date with a friend?

While we do not kick out the crutches, we do make allowances elsewhere. With a wink and a nod, we regularly move the pawns on the chessboards of our holier-than-thou lives so we can, with internal moral approval, speed dial the number to our workplaces and leave a voicemail message which will begin with, "I woke up sick today."

Historically, the church has been plagued with false ethics. Churchgoers often will go through a circular, internal conversation which begins with, "There is no problem in our congregation; we are of one mind and one spirit," followed by, "Satan has infiltrated our church with negative people who are doing the Devil's work among us."

If honesty prevailed, we would own our passive-aggressive behavior in the pews and admit we store our disgruntled and jumbled angry feelings.

That is, until the annual church business meeting when, with precision, we spiritually and verbally assassinate each other.

While delivering the Sermon on the Mount (see Matthew 5), Jesus described the church as the "salt of the earth" and the "light of the world." There was no hedging, no beating around the bush: Christ intended the church to be a glowing beacon of hope and redemption in a world continuously teetering on the precipice of despair. This wasn't to be an uncertain flame, but a bright light.

Bonhoeffer, in his famous work, *The Cost of Discipleship*, got in the church's face with his conclusion about the church's ultimate task: "The call of Jesus Christ means either that we are the salt of the earth, or else we are annihilated: either we follow the call or we are crushed beneath it. There is no question of a second chance."[2]

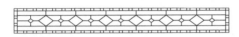

CHRIST INTENDED THE CHURCH TO BE A GLOWING BEACON OF HOPE AND REDEMPTION IN A WORLD CONTINUOUSLY TEETERING ON THE PRECIPICE OF DESPAIR.

Scripture is full of multiple warnings about the impact of internal chaos on a congregation. If we don't handle it well, it can destroy us. The problems come when individual parishioners get so intent with hearing their own voices they no longer seek God's plan and listen for His still small voice—the voice of the Almighty, the One in charge.

I have often been in the grandstands of Christendom, giving God high fives and standing ovations for His cameo appearances in my small world. Such a sad state of affairs. I realize I have spent far too much time looking in my mirror, and not nearly enough listening to God in His Word.

---

[2] Ibid, 117.

The church does an excellent job of memorizing God's laws for abundant living and citing His Son's recipe for righteousness, but the *ecclesia*[3] often fails God's ultimate message: The truth can hurt.

We run from hurt.

We assume that only the deranged choose pain. Perhaps some do, but we do not. However, whether it is anguish associated with childbirth, the pain of discovering a spouse who has broken a marital promise, or the heartache of the teenager who walks out the front door for the last time, real pain seems to be waiting in the wings of our tomorrows. Pain is a part of our lives, and we don't like it.

To avoid pain, we often choose to not tell each other the truth because we do not want to be confrontational. We assume Christians have never been given a celestial green light to be honest with each other. Instead we share a hymnal, smile when necessary, and hug others before leaving the sanctuary to fulfill the standard connectivity ritual of the faithful.

Contrary to the Word of God, we do not tell another disciple of Christ the truth because the truth *doesn't* set us free. Instead the truth will, based on our memories, often divide and doom the body of Christ.

So we smile and go underground with our honesty. The truth, we assume, will always be difficult. We think telling the truth means we have become unstable and are comfortable in creating havoc in our imperfect and flawed fellowship. Without the boldness to speak to our wobbling world, God through Jesus Christ, is pounding on the doors of our minds, hearts, and futures to touch us with fierce faith.

Our Lord is both gentle and aggressive. His gentle voice guides us as we stumble through the dark canyons of our painful nights and His aggressive love holds us tight.

---

[3] Greek word for the assembly that directs the church.

Elton Trueblood said, in his riveting book, *The Incendiary Fellowship,* "The renewal of the Church *(sic)* will be in progress when it is seen as a fellowship of consciously inadequate persons who gather ... with one another and with Christ who has made them bold."[4]

For the contemporary disciple of Jesus Christ, boldness does not result in running into the middle of a busy traffic intersection and screaming to passing vehicles, "You are all going to hell if you do not repent right now." Spiritual boldness is ultimately saying to God, "Ready or not, here I come."

It's that pristine moment when we mumble in prayer, "Lord, I have not earned the right to ask You to heal my mind/body/marriage, but because You have called me Your child, I boldly throw myself and my future into Your hands."

Salvation is the bold moment when we realize God knows not only our name, but also the worst, often tragic moments in our lives too. And God still chooses to glue Himself to us and refuses to walk out on us. God has always been aggressive about chasing us down the boulevards and small worn paths of our life. His love is relentless.

The English poet, Francis Thompson, penned these riveting words in his famous poem, "The Hound of Heaven":

"I fled Him, down the nights and down the days;
I fled Him, down the arches of the years;
I fled Him, down the labyrinthine ways
Of my own mind; and in the mist of tears I hid from Him..."[5]

Thompson captured, in words, the aggressive, unrelenting love of God.

---

[4] Elton Trueblood, *The Incendiary Fellowship* (New York: Harper & Row, 1978).

[5] Nicholson and Lee, Oxford book of English mystical verse (Clarendon Pr., 1917).

This is the "all-in" approach to life. I meet these people all the time. These are the devil-may-care folks who willfully jump into the gondola of a hot air balloon; ski down the black runs at Telluride, Colorado; or swim with sharks in Grand Cayman.

In the body of Christ, we struggle with taking spiritual risks. We keep reminding ourselves and those around us to just keep doing what we have been doing and saying what we have been saying. Because, if we digress from this celestial playbook, someone may get hurt.

So we do not tell each other the truth, because the truth may hurt someone or even the entire body of Christ.

The biblical history of nobodies who bumbled into the presence of God is pockmarked with divine aggressiveness. The thundering voice that accosted Moses in the desert, the quiet whisper in the middle of the night to a frightened, teenaged Mary and the Damascus road instructions bellowed to Saul, all communicated the Hound of Heaven was, and is, tracking us.

Salvation is definitive. The pursuing Prince of Peace does not mumble meaningless mantras and pious platitudes. The Son of God, Jesus of Nazareth, has been and will continue to pursue us.

Dorothy Sayers, the renowned English crime writer, poet and playwright wrote, "(Sloth) is the sin which believes in nothing, cares for nothing, seeks to know nothing, interferes with nothing, enjoys nothing, loves nothing, hates nothing, finds purpose in nothing, lives for nothing, and remains alive only because there is nothing to die for."[6]

Sayers has captured the essence of the anemic Christian: the card-carrying believer who totes around a small King James Bible and a poisonous

---

[6] Diane Singer, "Dorothy Sayers on Sloth," Dorothy Sayers on Sloth, February 6, 2008, accessed September 28, 2017, http://www.doingtherightthing.com/tp-home/blog-archives/blog-archives/entry/4/4408.

non-confrontational dose of religion as part of their résumé. You know, hang with the right people, frequent the right restaurants, know the right names to drop at the Christmas party, and continually keep the contacts on your cell phone up-to-date. We fit in. We do what everyone else does.

Unfortunately, we do not tell the truth to other Christians because we do not want to be labeled as a hyper-spiritual religious fanatic. The last moniker we want stamped on our foreheads is spiritual wacko, so we avoid any situation that smacks of a confrontation.

Why? We avoid telling another believer the truth because remaining neutral is always a safe harbor for religion. Becoming resolute, especially about issues of personal faith, has always proven to be dangerous, so we keep our religion normal. The abnormal (displayed with precision in the Bible) birthed a bumper crop of spiritual zealots who boldly stood in front of a card-carrying Pharaoh, or stood in a dusty Jerusalem street and screamed, *"These men are not drunk, as you suppose. It's only nine in the morning! No, this is what was spoken by the prophet Joel"* (Acts 2:15-16).

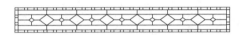

WE AVOID TELLING ANOTHER BELIEVER THE TRUTH BECAUSE REMAINING NEUTRAL IS ALWAYS A SAFE HARBOR FOR RELIGION.

Today, scrubbed, sanctified and silent religiosity keeps the church powerless in a high-stakes, constantly changing, megatrend world. Within the church, believers must move past the fear of telling the truth because the truth will ultimately "set us free" just as Jesus said it would in John 8:32.

Playwright George Bernard Shaw wrote, "This is the true joy of life, being used for a purpose recognized by yourself as a mighty one; being a force of nature instead of a feverish, selfish little clod of ailments and grievances complaining that the world will not devote itself to making you happy."[7]

The church will always be present. But, being present does not guarantee it will be relevant or powerful.

The inert, passive church was captured by the Beatles in "Eleanor Rigby": "Eleanor Rigby died in the church, and was buried along with her name. Nobody came. Father McKenzie, wiping the dirt from his hands, as he walks from the grave. No one was saved. All the lonely people, where do they all come from?"[8]

If Christians choose to not rock the boat, the people of the church become spiritual Stepford Wives: Everyone will be smiling at the right time to the right person, sipping a steaming hot latte and hoping no one will upset this ecclesiastical apple cart by telling each other the truth.

The church, I am convinced, will always be present. But the real question is, "Will the church be bold and viable?"

The people in the church are the first attractant.

The tangible expression of the church is the person next to us in a pew. The flesh and blood parts of our lives are on display in these long spiritual benches where we wrestle, as the first disciples did, to understand the brief, but clear words of our Lord, *"...Come, follow me..."* (Matt. 4:19).

With our brothers and sisters of faith nestled next to us, we need to be reminded that within the first three to six seconds of meeting a new person, we will psychologically slot them into a hanging file, nestled quietly between our ears.

---

[7] Greg Jones, PhD., ""Launched"," Westminster Presbyterian Church - Sermons & Bulletins, January 9, 2011, accessed September 28, 2017, http://www.wpc.org/sermons/detail/Launched/64.

[8] Lennon and McCartney, writers, Eleanor Rigby; Yellow submarine, Parlophone, 1966, CD.

Therefore, here are two questions for any congregation of believers: "Do people who have never believed God exist, find Him in these pews with us? Will they detect divinity in our words, in our worship, in our priorities and in our failures?"

Telling each other the truth, even when the truth hurts, authenticates our faith, dries our tears and surprisingly, teaches us how to dance.

Chapter Two

We Do Not Tell the Truth Because We Do Not Know How to "Speak the Truth in Love"

TELLING SOMEONE THE truth is always emotionally dicey. The truth can trigger a memory or sever a longstanding relationship.

Your choice of words, your tone of voice, any wrongdoing you may infer, and then your halting conclusions, may bring on a volcanic eruption of anger, regret, indignation, hurt, and insults, which can be topped off with a sticky silence that drips from every molecule hanging between the two of you.

Truth-telling is not for the faint of heart.

In the mid-1980s, I became a professional presenter for National Seminars Group headquartered in Kansas City, Missouri. To prepare for my six-hour presentations around the world and throughout the United States and Canada, I read a fascinating book, *Your Perfect Right,* by Alberti and Emmons.[9] In it, I found the skills I wished I had learned much earlier in my life.

---

9 Robert E. Alberti and Michael L. Emmons, *Your Perfect Right: a Guide to Assertive Behavior.* With forew. by John Vasconcellos(San Luis Obispo: IMPACT, 1975).

The book was built on a simple model of communication: when we send messages to each other, we choose from one of three ego states. You can decide, before sending and receiving messages with another person, if you will be the parent, the adult, or the child.

The *parent* is someone who will try to *control* their environment: its content and possible outcomes. The parent is intent on making sure they dominate all communication. They will control conversation with tone of voice, continuously interrupt the speaker's thoughts, and then undermine the solutions he or she did not create, belittling any new approaches that did not come from the parent.

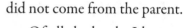

YOU CAN DECIDE, BEFORE SENDING AND RECEIVING MESSAGES WITH ANOTHER PERSON, IF YOU WILL BE THE PARENT, THE ADULT, OR THE CHILD.

Of all the books I have read about ego states, the parent was the most difficult to verbally engage. This individual begins most conversations with an emotional challenge, such as, "Since I am well read on this topic, we will not have to spend a lot of time finding additional information. Let's just move on to make a decision..."

The parent ego state makes dialogue difficult. At the end of any lecture, you almost expect the parent will say, "Now, go up and make your bed, brush and floss your teeth and clean up your bedroom since it looks like a landfill."

The child ego state, in contrast to the parent, will accomplish his goals by projecting weakness and seeking affirmation. A child may shower you with many "woe is me" statements: "I should have expected this response from you. You have never been on my side." "Sure, go ahead and make the decision without me. I'm used to that." "I have lived a very difficult life and our church adds to my agony."

Notice the child ego state is immersed in its own victimization. This person constantly reminds those around him he has a long and tragic history of being the weak and forgotten one in any crowd. Unfortunately, the child may remain stunted in emotional growth his entire life. This ego state results in the adult whiner.

There is a third ego state: the adult. We assume this one will be a cakewalk after meandering through the eccentricities of the parent and the child. Yes, the adult ego state should be the zenith of our humanity. This is when we are grown-up and mature and should have our stuff together. The adult is responsible.

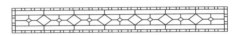

WE ARE LONGING FOR PEOPLE IN OUR LIVES WHO WILL TELL US THE TRUTH, REFUSE TO PLAY INTERPERSONAL, NON-VERBAL GAMES AND BE *ADULT* WHO WILL PUT US AT EASE WITH MATURITY.

At the same time, we know not all adults are "grown up." Do you have someone who hangs around in your family tree and has amassed a lifetime of birthdays but has never made it to maturity? You know, the perpetual teenager?

We are longing for people in our lives who will tell us the truth, refuse to play interpersonal, non-verbal games and be *adult* who will put us at ease with maturity.

The parent and child ego states have a mire of liabilities. We want the adult to ride into our organizational systems and dispense vast amounts of maturity and emotional peace.

So what does the parent, child, adult paradigm have to do with Christians telling each other the truth? Is there a specific ego state that impacts people of faith who are working at bringing unity to the body of Christ?

Let's work on the first question.

When we walk into a specific, sometimes not familiar, environment, we are choosing one of the three ego states which we are convinced will get us what we want.

If you decide the parent needs to make a cameo appearance, you will take control, be definitive about your expectations of everyone in the room, constantly remind everyone of your value, or end your time with them with a lecture about self-discipline because no one works or cares as much as you do.

The parent is this multi-faceted individual who will literally place his life on the line for someone who agrees with his view about almost everything, verbally clarify the rules for "living in my house," and then sit in a high-backed chair as he happily shares his history of outstanding accomplishments with anyone who will listen.

Normally the parent ego state does not work well with Christians.

Historically, the church devours itself every few years. Christendom has a long history of eating its own offspring, especially when the saints do not fulfill the parent's (priests, clergy, elders, denominational leaders) wishes.

Os Guinness, in his historic work, *The Dust of Death,* warned us about this in 1979 with this searing theological diatribe about the future of the church, when he said, "Meaning is no longer what God means about himself to man, but rather what man means as he searches for God and expresses himself in human terms."[10] The church is remaking itself in its own image instead of reflecting Christ. That can't turn out well.

The church mimics our culture: The liturgy gets shorter, the music gets louder, the Word gets homogenized and the call to confession gets diluted into Christianese. All of this is dispensed in waves of religious

---

[10] Os Guinness, *The Dust of Death: a Critique of the Counter Culture* (Inter-Varsity Press, Downers Grove, Ill., 1973).

pep rallies accented with surround-sound speakers and acres of projection space, using the latest screen innovations available.

There is nothing questionable about spiritual growth, but there is something terribly wrong when each congregation spends most of its time admiring itself and then comparing itself against the spiritual competitors down the street.

One of the reasons we do not tell each other the truth is that we have long histories of effectively using the parent ego state, which usually ends with "my way or the highway."

There is an ego-defense mechanism at work here that is the opposite of "loving one another." We defend our carefully constructed positions instead of working together. Here are four behaviors we normally pull off the shelf when we decide to be passive-aggressive.

We use *avoidance* to defend ourselves from uncomfortable people or environments. This emotional and verbal skill is quite simple. When we are stuck in a physical or emotional corral with a person whose voice, agenda, or belief system we find offensive or even awkward, we will find a way out. We look at our wristwatch, check our cell phone, or interrupt with "I just remembered something I have to do right now." All of these are acceptable passports for getting out of an uncomfortable situation. We get away from uncomfortable people and places by adopting passive-aggressive behaviors. These behaviors allow us to express hostility without using direct language. It's much less messy.

Abusing time is an effective way to passively express your aggressive thoughts and feelings. Someone can press your hot buttons by showing up late for an appointment or "time got away from me this morning" or "I guess I was preoccupied about some other pressing problems today. I will have to continue this conversation at another time."

This is a subtle game. Both parties know neither gets more or less hours in any given day. Because time is a nonrenewable resource, it can be used as a weapon. If you have ever waited for someone, who does not share your priorities about the effective use of time, you are acquainted with the feeling that you have been (passively) insulted by this person. Further it lets you know that whatever it was you were supposed to do with this person is not high on your list, therefore your relationship probably is not essential. The trouble with this method is that it's almost impossible to pin it down and bring an end to it. As a result, this relationship does not grow, but stagnates in its bed of excuses.

Learned helplessness is an excellent way to passively get what you want/ need from another person. These people say things like, "I don't know why I am not getting everything done today." "I do not have the information you wanted for this meeting because my life is just a living hell." "I am buried with 911 items on my to-do list today."

This poor-me syndrome is intended to elicit pity and buy more time, and it normally has a long history. Someone who uses this ploy has been rewarded in the past with a response like, "Hey, we all have bad days. Why don't you go home early today?"

How do we know that? Because we do not repeat behavior unless it is rewarded. Every time we excuse a reoccurring, negative behavior like learned helplessness, we guarantee this behavior will occur again in the near future.

Willful incompetence is a non-violent way of staying out of the fray. These people send this message: "You really do not want me to follow through on what you have asked me to do because I will probably screw-up everything again."

This "I-am-all-thumbs" person will drag you through his latest history of ineptitude. These unreliable people have crafted a reputation of masterful incompetence which will always get them exactly what they want: to be left alone.

Incompetence has always been a topic we lament and in which we find humor. George Bernard Shaw wrote, "Democracy substitutes election by the incompetent for the appointment by the corrupt few."[11]

Incompetence, when acknowledged, should change and morph into excellence. When the comfort of incompetence becomes more desirable than the results of excellence, our world gets dumbed-down and our lives become second-rate.

The Bible contains a unique requirement. We are to be truth-tellers and "speak the truth in love" (see Ephesians 4:15). Jesus told the truth to everyone He met, always reaching out to them and urging them to know His Father. He called His disciples to follow Him by sharing in His pain, His holiness, and His mission. His famous prayer was to ask God to *"...lead us not into temptation, but deliver us from the evil one"* (Matt. 6:13). This call was a gutsy one, and did not include the carrots of wealth, position and power. Instead Jesus expected His new disciples to understand, and then apply, the all-consuming love He gave them as the antidote for all expressions of evil.

Love is such a plastic word in our nanosecond world. You can love your dog, your job, the weather today, the nine-iron shot you made when approaching a difficult green and...the list goes on. Love is also an emotionally-charged noun/verb which we use to splash the right flavor into our lives. After all, if you are not a lover, you will slowly digress to become the next Ebenezer Scrooge.

After sitting through Erich Segal's sweaty love extravaganza, *Love Story*, with Oliver Barrett IV and Jennifer Cavalleri whispering to each other,

---

[11] "George Bernard Shaw Quotes," BrainyQuote, accessed September 28, 2017, https://www.brainyquote.com/quotes/quotes/g/georgebern109536.html.

"Love means never having to say you are sorry...." we are often flummoxed by love. Love is here today and tragically... gone tomorrow.

Scripture, on the other hand, is replete with another description of love:

"For God so loved... that He gave..." (John 3:16).

"Greater love has no one than this: to lay down one's life for one's friends" (John 15:13).

"Love is patient, love is kind. It does not envy, it does not boast, it is not proud" (1 Cor. 13:4).

This brand of love confuses us. If we love, we expect something in return. Unrequited love is a downer and has the same shelf-life as last week's meatloaf: here today and gone tomorrow. If we show love to another human being, we become angry and frustrated if we receive nothing in return.

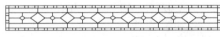

TO PROVE HIS AFFECTION, HE WRAPPED HIMSELF IN OUR FLESH.

The bottom-line message of Bethlehem is God, the Creator of the universe, decided to lavishly love all of us, despite our failures, faults and faithlessness.

Whether or not we are holy, nice, Republican, environmentalist, Methodist, holy-roller or voted most "likely to succeed" in high school, God took the initiative to individually love every last one of us. To prove His affection, He wrapped Himself in our flesh.

This divine decision created a puzzle for us. We cruise through our egocentric personalized worlds, laughing, learning, taking cell phone pictures ad infinitum; and we still go to bed every night and review the reams of reasons why we are unlovable.

Nelson Mandela, a man who confounded an angry, seething world with his meek silence said, "I am not a saint, unless you think of a saint as a sinner who keeps on trying."[12]

This repetitious trying is our way of not giving up on our potential for salvation.

The apostle Paul addressed this spiritual assumption in his letter to the church at Ephesus, *"But because of his great love for us, God, who is rich in mercy, made us alive with Christ even when we were dead in transgressions— it is by grace you have been saved"* (Eph. 2:4-5).

If you have recently reminded yourself of how totally unfit you are to be a follower of Jesus Christ, repeat these words: "It is by grace I have been saved."

Our world continuously taunts us with that quiet whisper in the middle of the night, "You are not working hard enough at your job, your marriage, your relationships with your children, your stock portfolio, your weight...."

We are often our worst enemy. We have so many missing pieces in our fractured lives and so many failures to page through between our ears, we have convinced ourselves we could never be loved, especially if the person who loves us is the Creator of the universe.

Christians do not tell each other the truth because truth will only remind us of how handicapped we are in our pathetic holiness.

But Ephesians 2:4-5 is not about us. Grace is all about Him, not the person in our mirror. If we acquire just a covering of God's grace, our

---

[12] Jack Williams Valerie Lawhorn, "Nelson Mandela's 1999 Speech At Rice Remembered," Houston Public Media, December 05, 2013, accessed October 18, 2017, https://www.houstonpublicmedia. org/articles/news/2013/12/05/48064/nelson-mandelas-1999-speech-at-rice-remembered/.

worlds will be decorated with the ambiance of a limitless love which is here today and will be in all of our tomorrows.

We need a true revelation of God's love, deeply rooted in our hearts and minds. Then when the angst of a difficult tomorrow bounces off the grace of God, we can tell the truth and the truth will set us free to learn how to love ourselves. It is only after we have learned to love the person in our mirror that speaking the truth in love becomes God's next miracle.

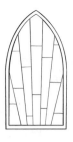

CHAPTER THREE

WE DO NOT TELL THE TRUTH BECAUSE WE DO NOT WANT TO CREATE CONFLICT IN THE CHURCH

CHRISTIANS OFTEN LIE to each other.

Have you asked a fellow believer, "How are you doing on this beautiful Sunday morning?" and heard this response, "I am having a great day in spite of the appeal for the building fund this morning. Isn't God good?"

Those words have the makings of a lethal religious cocktail. The, "I am having a great day..." was intended to soften up the listener to drop the 500-pound verbal bomb ("...in spite of the appeal for the building fund").

Every pew is populated with people who own an opinion which has the potential to create interpersonal conflict. What we do not know and accept is conflict can be an asset.

There is nothing wrong with conflict. Conflict can be a healthy sign. It means there is life and vitality in the body of Christ. Lethargy, not conflict, is the ultimate threat to a healthy expression of the *ecclesia*.

Over the centuries, the church has repeatedly damaged its credibility before a watching world. It has done this with its wide smiles, fifteen-pound

Bibles, unabashed public "amens" and unsolicited diatribes about dancing, dogma and maybe the Democrats.

With great gusto, the church has worked hard to establish its own expression of the community of faith: one that is populated with the right brothers and sisters who enthusiastically endorse the same creed. From the Crusades to today's religious wars battling it out on any one of the 130 satellite channels of our big-screen television sets, the church has always been a raging cauldron of often undefined and competitive religiosity.

C.S. Lewis captured the essence of the church when he said, "I believe there are too many practitioners in the church who are not believers."[13]

The church drips with the residue of a man-made religion, devoid of hope. Lying, cheating, unbridled anger, disillusionment, hostility and quick retaliation slathers our evening news with the bad news among the good news people. And the church is not exempt from our society's rampant selfishness either. We often drag all our fear and resentment for each other to the altar.

A. W. Tozer described the paradox between the church and its calling when he wrote, "One hundred religious persons knit into a unity by careful organization do not constitute a church any more than eleven dead men make a football team. The first requisite is life, always."[14]

Life should come before our religion. Sitting in the presence of the King of Kings and Lord of Lords affects us. We may not be perfect, but we are clearly working on receiving divine Life over the wasteland of our wanderings.

---

[13] C. S. Lewis, "C. S. Lewis on Hypocrisy," Christian Quotes, accessed October 18, 2017, http://christian-quotes.ochristian.com/christian-quotes_ochristian.cgi?find=Christian-quotes-by-C.S.Lewis-on-Hypocrisy.

[14] A. W. Tozer, "The Communion of Saints," A. W. Tozer: Man - The Dwelling Place of God, accessed October 18, 2017, https://www.worldinvisible.com/library/tozer/5j00.0010/5j00.0010.19.htm.

The litmus test of our commitment to make Christ the Lord of our lives may be whether or not we have the spiritual fortitude to tolerate and show respect for the person seated next to us in church. This flawed believer may be your greatest spiritual challenge, but it is in those relationships Christ's love becomes a pragmatic evidence of his presence.

A question seeps through this in the end: "When I have conflict with another disciple of Jesus Christ, how do I resolve the anger and distance I feel between the two of us?"

There are four initiatives all of us need to activate when grace-filled believers like us fail.

First, remind yourself the Word of God is soaked in sin. From the forbidden fruit of Eden to the skinny-dipping of King David, to the screaming, antagonistic Corinthians at their church business meetings, hordes of the faithful all through history have willfully and tragically failed. The early church is the mother lode of the church's errors and mistakes. Look at James when he describes the immaturity of this congregation with these honest words, *"You*

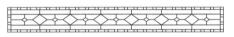

THIS FLAWED BELIEVER MAY BE YOUR GREATEST SPIRITUAL CHALLENGE, BUT IT IS IN THOSE RELATIONSHIPS CHRIST'S LOVE BECOMES A PRAGMATIC EVIDENCE OF HIS PRESENCE.

desire but do not have, so you kill. You covet but you cannot get what you want, so you quarrel and fight. You do not have because you do not ask God. When you ask, you do not receive, because you ask with wrong motives, that you may spend what you get on your pleasures. You adulterous people, don't you know that friendship with the world means enmity with God? ...Submit yourselves, then, to God. Resist the devil, and he will flee from you. Come near to God and he will draw near to you. Wash your hands, you sinners, and purify your hearts, you double-minded" (James 4:2-4, 7-8).

Conflict is addressed in the fabric of our faith. Besides the biblical scenes of Moses smashing the Ten Commandments, the instructions God gave us on how to live at peace with each other, our hymnology is filled with multiple calls for unity in the body of Christ. Songs like "Bind Us Together," "In Christ There Is No East or West," and "The Church's One Foundation" are examples.

Conflict, in or outside the church, has defined parameters. Our tendency to oppose and then demean each other has been studied by behavioral therapists and theologians for centuries. There are five stages of conflict.

Conflict is always ignited when someone, with whom you regularly worship, non-verbally communicates, "I do not need you or your affirmation to be okay."

We will often write people out of our spiritual and personal futures when we communicate these five basic non-verbal messages:

"I will never change the reputation I have crafted for myself. You must accept me as I am."

"I will never share power with you."

"I will never submit to putting myself in what I perceive to be a losing position."

"I will never allow you or anyone else to have control of my life."

"I will tell you exactly what I think and feel and I do not care if you approve or not."

"Losing face" is all about the rapid evaporation of our self-image. The Persian King Xerxes had a stellar military career until he met Greek resistance at Plataea and the Persian invasion was decisively quelled. James II of England lost face quickly in his short three-year reign when William III and Mary II made his reign a fleeting memory. Captain Edward Smith of the Titanic had a perfect life and career until he called out, "Full speed ahead," and raced his ship right into an iceberg.

All these historic heroes would never have made a choice to denigrate a reputation. A stellar reputation has always been the first step to greatness.

Losing power is the next stage after losing face.

Power is a most satisfying elixir to anyone who has tasted the sweet delight of telling someone, "I need this done immediately" and watched as people moved quickly to obey.

Napoleon Bonaparte said, "I love power. But it is as an artist that I love it. I love it as a musician loves his violin, to draw out its sounds and chords and harmonies."[15] Bonaparte was observed by those in his realm as euphoric when reviewing the spoils of his conquests.

Next, losing a position normally means, "I will not change regardless of how angry and disappointed people are with me right now." When "organizational power" is lost or diminished, there is normally someone with tons of positional power, who will slam doors shut and terminate anyone who harbors a different opinion than theirs.

What follows the loss of a position is losing influence.

We see this mentality in movers and shakers. These people have quietly memorized the flow chart of an organization and then aggressively identified the king-makers. With boundless enthusiasm, the movers and shakers

---

[15] "Napoleon Bonaparte Quotes," BrainyQuote, accessed October 18, 2017, https://www.brainyquote.com/quotes/quotes/n/napoleonbo150182.html.

strategically kiss up to those who can fuel their star power. Needless to say, these people leave a trail of conflict and tears in their wake.

The final stage of initiating conflict is sending the message: "You do not have the right to expect me to listen to you."

There is nothing more dehumanizing than to have someone let you know the following: "You are not an essential person in my life; therefore, I do not have the time or interest to listen to you." It's no surprise this individual will create chaos in a faith-based community.

Conflict precipitates any of these assumptions. Honestly, there are people who have no inner desire to change their feelings. They are obsessed with nurturing their quiet anger and pervasive need to control. They feel justified in their actions.

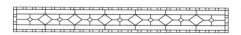

WE DO NOT TELL EACH OTHER THE TRUTH BECAUSE WE DO NOT WANT TO BECOME THAT 500 POUNDS OF SPIRITUAL TNT WHICH WILL BLOW UP THE BODY OF CHRIST.

It is important to note feelings are not right or wrong— they are just present. Assertive, healthy believers in Christ and His Word are individuals who own their feelings and can represent them with clarity. Therefore, the antidote for conflict among disciples of Jesus Christ is a healthy dose of truth-telling.

We do not tell each other the truth because we do not want to become that 500 pounds of spiritual TNT which will blow up the Body of Christ. In our spiritual scrapbooks, we have seen the aftermath of spiritual explosions. We have seen them rip apart, limb by limb, a body of believers who, like Humpty Dumpty, could not be put back together again. So how does the Church inoculate itself against the next infestation of conflict among the faithful?

Look closely at these four practical steps.

First, let's review the biblical remedy for a congregation writhing in internal strife. The apostle James wrote to the infantile body of Christ throughout Asia Minor during the first century. After reading his short letter, it is obvious James was frustrated with churches that did not have the time or energy to build the kingdom of God because they were exhausted from picking fights with each other.

Sound familiar?

The worst public relations factor that will doom any congregation is the constant bickering behind the church doors. James addressed these jousting Jesus junkies with these words: *"Consider it pure joy, my brothers and sisters, whenever you face trials of many kinds, because you know that the testing of your faith produces perseverance...Everyone should be quick to listen, slow to speak and slow to become angry, because human anger does not produce the righteousness that God desires. Therefore, get rid of all moral filth and the evil that is so prevalent and humbly accept the word planted in you, which can save you"* (James 1:2-3, 19b-21).

If you are looking for a spiritual paradigm to address a difficult, often obnoxious believer in your spiritual life, notice the three directions James recommended: *"quick to listen," "slow to speak,"* and *"slow to become angry."* Let's look more closely at each of these divine disciplines.

Being *slow to speak* is not easy, especially when you are normally not stumped for words. You may need a step-by-step plan to assist you. Here's some suggestions:

Identify your hot buttons.

Here are some of the words that may light my spiritual fire: "You are kidding me...you call yourself a Christian." "Sure. I will be happy to repeat my spiritual concerns again...assuming you can understand God's Word." Or, "I am praying for you because you obviously are not listening to what our Lord is telling you."

Take a few moments right now to write down all the words that can leave you with vast reservoirs of seething anger.

With practice and intentional prayer, we can choose to remain calm in emotionally heated moments, remembering who we serve. You may mentally recite: "Christ is Lord of my life and my words. I will represent my Lord in the words I choose and the tone I convey. I will not allow my anger or passions to supersede God's will. I will respond and not react."

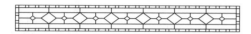

WITH PRACTICE AND INTENTIONAL PRAYER, WE CAN CHOOSE TO REMAIN CALM IN EMOTIONALLY HEATED MOMENTS, REMEMBERING WHO WE SERVE.

Second, when you have emotional control, ask the other person to meet you at a specific time and place. Make sure at least a full day passes before this meeting. You will need this time to strategize your thoughts and pray for control of your emotions.

Third, write out a "sequential list of statements" you want to use to begin the conversation. Additionally, suggest to the other person both of you can make written notes as the conversation progresses. Your intent is to capture factual statements and information for the next stage.

Fourth, and I know this sounds time-consuming, after the two of you have expressed your thoughts, feelings and spiritual expectations, agree to meet again. Choose a date and place within the next three days when the two of you will get back together to continue your conversation.

These interim days will provide both of you with the privacy to absorb and pray about the best response for the words and feelings each of you heard and observed.

Fifth, a final meeting should be planned to wrap up the conflict. In this meeting the goal is that both of you be transparent, listening, kind, and supportive of one another. If one of you is not comfortable with the progress you anticipated, another meeting should take place.

Our psyche is a well-tuned alarm system. When the bells between your ears start pealing, have a quick conversation with yourself and state the obvious, *I cannot control the person seated in front of me. The only person I can manage and control is me.* Most importantly, breathing a short prayer for divine help at this emotionally charged moment is a spiritual necessity.

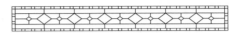

UNRESOLVED CONFLICT IS THE GREATEST THREAT TO BUILDING THE KINGDOM OF GOD AMONG US.

If you cannot control your words, thoughts and emotional balance, take a break. That's right. Look at the other person and say, "I want to respond to you, but I will need a few minutes alone to prioritize all I am thinking and feeling right now."

Let's stop for a minute and recount this foundational assumption: Conflict is a given in all our tomorrows, and conflict afflicts, like every other organization, even the church.

Unresolved conflict is the greatest threat to building the kingdom of God among us.

Regardless of denominational affiliation, no faith community can be "salt and light" in a watching world if the pews are full of strife.

Alexander Strauch wrote, "There is nothing wrong with a Christian disagreeing with one another or trying to persuade another of the rightness of a particular position. What is wrong, however, is loveless conflict that ends in hate and bitterness."[16]

---

[16] Alexander Strauch, "Gracequotes.org," Grace Quotes, accessed October 18, 2017, https://gracequotes.org/topic/conflict-church/.

The loveless conflict was addressed by Christ in the Sermon on the Mount when He poured the foundation of the church He was building with words like:

> *"Blessed are the pure in heart, for they will see God"* (Matt. 5:8).

> *"Blessed are the poor in spirit, for theirs is the kingdom of heaven"* (Matt. 5:3).

> *"Blessed are the peacemakers, for they will be called children of God"* (Matt. 5:9).

Each of these three beatitudes confronts conflict within the body of Christ.

"Blessed are the pure in heart" directly confronts the need to resolve and dissolve conflict within the church. Malachy McCourt wrote, "Resentment is like taking poison and waiting for the other person to die."[17]

When we scan the pews in front of us and suddenly identify a saint who we believe has quietly, but effectively, attacked us with words and silence, our knee-jerk response is to strike back. So, we quietly sneak into our private arsenal where we stash our lethal words and lists of accusations, and roam through the vaults of acerbic feelings as we plan our next attack. When the moment is right, we will even this score.

---

[17] Alex Witchel, "AT LUNCH WITH: Malachy McCourt -- How a Rogue Turns Himself Into a Saint; The Blarney Fails to Hide an Emotional Directness," The New York Times, July 28, 1998, accessed October 18, 2017, http://www.nytimes.com/1998/07/29/books/lunch-with-malachy-mccourt-rogue-turns-himself-into-saint-blarney-fails-hide.html.

The reason we do not tell each other the truth is the truth can be an incendiary device. Once the conflagration begins, as we have witnessed in the past, there is no stopping the process of dehumanizing and demeaning each other.

Notice the power of the next beatitude. *"Blessed are the poor in spirit."*

On face value, we read these words as an endorsement by Christ that everyone in the kingdom of God should agree to be a spiritual pauper. When we study this passage though, we find that *"poor in spirit"* describes the relationship between the sinner and the Savior. The Word is not suggesting we become spiritually poor. Jesus is saying the poor understands and receives the undeserved grace that has been poured over the believer because he or she is an object of God's aggressive and everlasting love. The point? Conflict does not have a chance of survival in the cauldron of God's grace. Conflict, then, is not terminal.

The church debates, argues, negotiates, and listens to God's voice through the proclamation of the Word and then the *ecclesia* is invited to experience unity with the different people in the same pew. In other words, *"the poor in spirit"* means that we, the followers of Jesus Christ, are wowed into the kingdom of God because even though we are all paupers, we have been made rich through His grace.

The final beatitude above is *"Blessed are the peacemakers, for they will be called children of God"* (Matt. 5:9). Becoming a peacemaker is tantamount to addressing and dissolving conflict in the body of Christ. Isaiah 55:8 reminds us God's ways are not our ways. This Old Testament adage offers the final explanation of why people of the cross have difficulty telling each other the truth. When conflict is present, the assumption is that not everyone is reading the same Bible, praying to the same God, or following the same Lord.

The result of becoming a peacemaker is to be initiated into this celestial society (the children of God). In other words, we establish our spiritual credentials by choosing to become a peacemaker.

The psalmist penned these words, *"I will proclaim the Lord's decree: He said to me, 'You are my son; today I have become your father'"* (Psa. 2:7).

In John, we are invited to savor these words, *"Believe in the light while you have the light, so that you may become children of the light..."* (John 12:36a).

Resolving conflict is difficult, time-consuming, and often requires additional effort. One of the reasons we do not want to tell the truth is because we want harmony and nothing but smiles between the saints. Unfortunately, because we are all sinners saved by grace, harmony can be elusive...but never impossible.

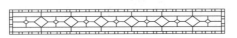

WE ESTABLISH OUR SPIRITUAL CREDENTIALS BY CHOOSING TO BECOME A PEACEMAKER.

The church must live with its smelly, unpredictable, often crass, humanity parked in the pews. We are not yet walking the streets of gold yet, but the last choice we want to make is to continually avoid telling each other the truth before we get there.

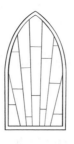

Chapter Four

We Do Not Tell the Truth Because We Cannot Trust Our Control of Words and Emotions

ALL OF US have horrid images, teeming between our ears, of a moment when we lost it in a confrontational conversation. You know, the other person was wrong and, without any mental or emotional hesitation, you were absolutely and completely right. You may have wanted to unload on this person with articulate precision and indignant emotions, and you did...especially if people nearby watched.

This individual, you decided, needed to be verbally reprimanded for all the world to see. And you assigned yourself as the perfect combatant that could clearly lay the charges in the open and then deliver the *coupe de grâce* with a final thrust of words like, "...and you know I am right."

We all avoid conflict. The last thing you said to yourself on your way to work yesterday was, "Wow, I cannot wait to go head-to-head with that disgusting person who insulted me in the staff meeting yesterday. I'll do it in front of everyone in the break room."

This approach would lead to either an announcement of the termination of your job or the first day of an all-expense paid trip into Workplace Hell.

Our approach to conflict is normally passive, which means we ignore it. We structure our days to spend most of our time with happy/friendly people who make us laugh, affirm our value, and bring us homemade brownies.

Despite our best efforts at avoidance, conflict does exist and has the potential to ruin a perfectly good day or life. When we accept the inevitability of conflict, we must choose a practical method to confront and resolve the awful prospect of picking fights with each other.

Let's begin by defining conflict.

The Merriam-Webster Dictionary definition includes these words, "... mental struggle resulting from incompatible or opposing needs, drives, wishes, or external or internal demands."[18] This definition means conflict will normally result in a headache, a stomachache, a backache or a life-ache.

Dr. Martin Luther King Jr. put together these eloquent words about finding peace in conflict, "True peace is not merely the absence of tension: It is the presence of justice."[19]

Conflict, left alone, will strip the human spirit of its greatness and then conclude with the haunting reality that conflict remains alive and well... right into our graves.

---

[18] "Conflict," Merriam-Webster, accessed October 20, 2017, https://www.merriam-webster.com/dictionary/conflict.

[19] Martin Luther King, Jr., "A quote by Martin Luther King Jr.," Quote by Martin Luther King Jr.: "True peace is not merely the absence of tension...", accessed October 20, 2017, https://www.goodreads.com/quotes/202045-true-peace-is-not-merely-the-absence-of-tension-it.

So what steps should the People of the Book take to avoid the liabilities of conflict and apply the verbal, emotional, and spiritual skills needed to effectively change this possible bit of trouble into an asset?

The first choice we must make before we confront conflict is to decide if we will be an introvert or an extrovert.

In the book, *Primal Leadership*, by Goleman, Boyatzis and McKee, the authors discuss the effects of how people feel about working in any organization that can account for twenty to thirty percent of their daily performance.[20] If we are not internally engaged in the product/service we are producing, along with the people sitting next to us, the potential consumer can easily detect our internal lack of a genuine support for our company or product.

Let's apply this proven fact to our continuous choice to be introversive or extroversive in a place of worship.

The introverted personality is comfortable working alone, driving alone, eating alone, and often living alone. This behavioral style values silence and quiet, and has little or no interest in resolving uncomfortable interpersonal relationships. When conflict appears, this personality style will withdraw and rarely, if ever, confront the conflict because, in his opinion, "...all of this will get out of control."

In the same situation, the extrovert will roll up his sleeves and loudly communicate, "People, people, we need to suck it up, face our disagreements, then get into our assigned small groups and hammer out a solution. We do not have time for being self-absorbed or pointing fingers. We have work to do here."

Sound familiar?

---

[20] Daniel Goleman, Annie McKee, and Richard Boyatzis, *Primal Leadership: Realizing the Power of Emotional Intelligence* (Brighton, Massachusetts: Harvard Business Review Press, 2002).

If you have been in a church for more than a few years you know all about the caustic beginnings of conflict and how this malady seeps into the sinews of the congregation. From the choice of the color for the sanctuary carpeting to whether or not the senior pastor should be granted a reserved parking place, there will always be conflict.

Internal strife always has been the greatest threat to the church. Church history is full of stories of congregations that grew at amazing speeds, only to hit the wall of unresolved internal conflict and stumble into tired worship, empty pews, and poor relationships in the group. But there is a cost for avoiding conflict. Like cancer, conflict can slowly and pervasively eat away at the health of the body if left unchecked. If a body of believers chooses to ignore the growing presence of conflict, the problem will infect the entire body.

The signs of conflict include silent messages echoing through the pews which usually end with, "Despite the expertise of our choir, the public speaking skills of our clergy and our fresh coffee, there is still something terribly wrong in this congregation."

What might that be? Well, Christians are not telling each other the truth. And the reason these folks of faith are mute about communicating with candor is their fear that when conflict resolution skills are employed, the saints will emotionally lose control and start fighting like undisciplined children who did not get what they wanted. They've seen it happen.

When we read the Bible, we confront the reality of our humanity, and one of the emotions which the Bible consistently addresses is anger. Paul did not hesitate to deal with the practical and spiritual implications of anger in the church. In writing to the church in Ephesus, Paul had this to say: *"In your anger do not sin: Do not let the sun go down while you are still angry, and do not give the devil a foothold"* (Eph. 4:26-27). Paul followed this with: *"Do not let any unwholesome talk come out of your mouths, but only what is helpful for building others up according to their needs, that it may benefit those who listen. And do not grieve the Holy Spirit of God, with whom you were sealed for the day of redemption. Get rid of all bitterness, rage and anger, brawling and slander, along with every form of malice"* (Eph. 4:29-31).

Paul made three main points here: (1) anger is a legitimate human emotion, intended to protect the individual and the church, (2) anger can become a willful decision to ignore the supernatural promise of peace provided by God for the believer, (3) there are long-term spiritual and emotional disadvantages if anger is held onto by Christians for extended periods of time.

The apostle James follows these conclusions with this wisdom, *"My dear brothers and sisters, take note of this: Everyone should be quick to listen, slow to speak and slow to become angry, because human anger does not produce the righteousness that God desires"* (James 1:19-20).

Ecclesiastes reminds us, *"Do not be quickly provoked in your spirit, for anger resides in the lap of fools"* (Ecc. 7:9).

With this clear biblical teaching about how to monitor and control anger, Christians have specific responsibilities.

If you are holding back or refusing to tell another Christian the truth, you probably are concerned that you cannot control your emotions. Your worst fear is you will lose control of your words, your body, and your reputation. This is a legitimate concern because when we lose emotional control, we also lose emotional and spiritual credibility.

Here are five sequential interventions you can use when you decide to confront conflict, but do not know how to navigate this emotionally-soaked environment.

First, suggest the time and place for this conversation. If you take the initiative to set up a face-to-face meeting, you will walk into the room with the credibility of the assertive leader. This suggestion has nothing to do with establishing power, but everything with giving yourself the right to initiate and outline the process of defining a mutually acceptable resolution. That's okay. In fact, it is healthy.

Another small, but essential, part of controlling this meeting is the physical arrangement of the environment. If you can, arrive first and arrange the chairs without a table between the two of you, and so you are not directly facing each other. This seating arrangement will eliminate a emotionally intimidating facing off positioning with the other person. If you sit directly in front of the other person, you assert the non-verbal message, "I have the right to be antagonistic and I want you to know I am in control right now." You want to avoid that.

Second, begin with a question, not a statement. The question could be, "Thank you for your time today. What are you expecting will be the outcome of our conversation?"

Notice the words expecting and outcome. Let's deal with reality: Neither of you probably wants to be in this room. If you hand this person the option of defining the end result of the meeting, then the two of you have a goal, not a position. That's a better starting place.

Third, continue to provide a comfortable emotional atmosphere by maintaining eye contact. Your eyes are the most expressive part of your body. We can tell if someone is sad, angry, relaxed, uptight, delighted, hopeless, or embarrassed by looking at his eyes. We often communicate without words with great clarity when we meet with coworkers, children, lovers, fellow believers and enemies. Think about the expressions you meet if you show up late with any of those people just mentioned. You are going to know what they think without them ever saying a word, by their eye contact, posture, and tone of voice when they say, "You better have a good excuse."

When we meet each other, always begin by giving the person "intermittent eye contact." Remember, sustained eye contact is emotionally threating and will create emotional space, confusion, and fear. When we stare, we alienate.

Fourth, when you disagree, admit it. You're allowed to disagree. People of faith live with the assumption they must agree to be liked and accepted. None of us wants to be relegated to the difficult person file, but if we disagree and choose not to be honest about the real reasons why we were angry or feeling alienated or frustrated, the relationship becomes difficult to maintain.

When you do not agree, use an assertive response like this: "When I reviewed the giving record of our congregation, I do not agree with the conclusion that our parishioners will vote with their wallets if they do not like our new pastor. Here are the reasons for my opinion." Most of us are excellent at reading eye contact and body language. If

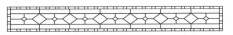

QUIETLY HARBORING DISAGREEMENT IS THE WORST CHOICE.

you have ever been in a church business meeting when a suggestion was made by someone on the board to initiate a new stewardship program, you probably heard silence. This silence is not golden. Instead it is a silent, but deafening, scream of enough is enough.

In any organization, quietly harboring disagreement is the worst choice. Appropriately stating what you think and feel is the ultimate expression of respect. If I do not respect you, your ideas, your leadership or your ministry, this disrespect will bleed through my words, eye contact, attendance, giving, even the strength of my handshake at the front door.

Fifth, when you do not get what you wanted, use your spirituality to let go. This is one of the benefits of grace. Throughout my life I have detested losing at anything, but I have still experienced loss. I lost as the pitcher in a championship Little League game in 1953 in Atco, New Jersey. I lost that young lady in Mainland Regional High School who would have been a perfect match for me, although she did not share this opinion.

But, I am not a loser. I am not, and neither are you. I am not someone constantly victimized by my sad-and-tragic life.

Life is unpredictable. None of us are promised a pain-free ride into eternity. Because I have met God Almighty through His Son, Jesus Christ, my confidence and genuine internal peace in the middle of my personal hell is that I am and will be okay.

Paul was often plagued by disappointment, and he made this declaration, *"For I am convinced that neither death nor life, neither angels nor demons, neither the present nor the future, nor any powers, neither height nor depth, nor anything else in all creation, will be able to separate us from the love of God that is in Christ Jesus our Lord"* (Rom. 8:38-39).

So, you and I, will continue to bumble around through the common happenings of life with its good days and, sometimes, very bad days. Our faith becomes the life preserver which we wear into today's challenges and tomorrow's disappointments. We, believers in the power and love of Jesus Christ, can tell each other the truth because the Truth will always guarantee a new sunrise even though yesterday may have been a trip through our own dark hell.

Remember, the key discipline in this chapter is control. To be disciples of Jesus Christ, we must always submit our thoughts and words to Him, and exercise self-control.

I know a lot about the popular weight control corporation, Weight Watchers, Inc. I have never worked for them or used their methodologies or product line, but I have met their believers. One personality trait seems to guarantee their success when stepping on that unforgiving scale. You can eat the right foods, exercise until you throw up, and enlist the help of family members who can identify the beginning of a binge. The one kill, though, that will always make the numbers on that scale head south is internal control.

We all have the same foundational choice: We must control our worst appetites. We do not tell the person next to us in the pew the truth because the truth will require us to acquire control over our worst vices. We are hesitant to tell the truth about our weaknesses because people of the kingdom should be in total control of all areas of our lives.

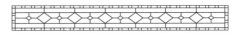

WE ARE HESITANT TO TELL THE TRUTH ABOUT OUR WEAK-NESSES BECAUSE PEOPLE OF THE KINGDOM SHOULD BE IN TOTAL CONTROL OF ALL AREAS OF OUR LIVES.

Here are the six categories of our lives where we struggle finding and then applying control: Thoughts, Prejudice, Assumptions, Motivations, Conclusions and Spirituality.

Thoughts: No one can tell what scenes, sounds, and secrets are continuously cascading over the movie screens of our minds. This is a private place where only one person has the ability to begin and end these thoughts. Not all our hidden musings center on murder, mischief and mayhem. As children of God, we are part of this startling process too: "Let the mind of Christ dwell in you."

How would you label your thought life? Is it fearful, sluggish, or out of control? If you answered yes to one of those adjectives, listen carefully to what the Word declares about the vitality of our minds: *"For the Spirit God gave us does not make us timid, but gives us power, love and self-discipline"* (2 Tim. 1:7).

The result of structuring a healthy mind was captured in the Paul's quote, *"Do not conform to the pattern of this world, but be transformed by the renewing of your mind. Then you will be able to test and approve God's will is — his good, pleasing and perfect will"* (Rom. 12:2). This transforming of my mind is a process, not a destination. Each day there is another nip 'n cut taking place between my ears as I learn to live the life God has planned for me.

Prejudice: When we think of prejudice, our thoughts turn to geographic location, skin color, political parties, particular automobiles, and so on. The list is endless.

The art of the deal in our culture is to find out as much information about a potential shopper and then send electronic carrots to their cell phone or computer which will make the product seem absolutely irresistible. So we purchase yet another product we do not need.

Prejudice soaks our society and our choices. We have all been infected with a desire to make those absolutely essential purchases.

What about prejudice and faith? Do we drag our prejudice into our prayer? Do we support a person in prayer because she thinks, believes and lives like us? Do we spiritually withdraw from people who do not share our beliefs?

Assumptions: We often do not encourage or listen to people who do not look and think like us. Despite our inquiring minds, hefty bank accounts, and good Internet dexterity, we harbor predetermined assumptions in our hearts and minds which have probably been hanging around for decades. We often do not tell each other the truth because we know, without a doubt, we have legions of iron-clad observations, which means our assumptions are valid and true. This is a heart issue in the church. The church can swing wide the front doors to the sanctuary until...the pews begin to fill up with people who do not share our particular beliefs or politics.

Motivations: Some people are annually motivated to clean out all their closets. Others find satisfaction in money. Still others are quietly euphoric when relatives call to say they will not be able to stop by tonight. Life is a highway of options and we keep coming back to the same doors, trying to pry them open...again and hoping the right door will open. Motivation, over time, creates this Pavlovian syndrome in all of us. We keep hitting our head against a motionless wall of our own assumptions that never change.

The only downside to motivation is it will change over time. Emotions do not jazz us today the way they did yesterday. Money, sex, organizational power, dinner at the White House, and a new car eventually becomes old hat. The mature Christian is someone who knows the moment of ultimate fulfillment is not the next generation car, the latest watch, or a new pair of running shoes. They don't live for prestige or the feeling one gets when addressing thousands of people either. The seasoned saint will jump off the not-so-merry merry-go-round of a hectic life and seek out a quiet place where he can hear *"Come to me, all of you who are weary and burdened, and I will give you rest"* (Matt. 11:28).

Conclusions:

Here is what we know about life, faith and controlling our words and emotions:

1. Our families are a collection of sometimes difficult people who will test our faith.

2. If you take care of your body, you also take care of your mind.

3. Time management is what we complain about, but seldom fix.

4. When push comes to shove, most of us will embrace the truth, especially when we are in pain.

5. God might be disappointed with us, but His limitless love keeps Him from using His eraser when looking at our name in the Book of Life.

6. We expect too much perfection from ourselves and from each other.

7. Money makes us happy for about...five minutes.

8. As we grow up, regardless of our age, we will one day stumble onto the promise that God is, indeed, the Hound of Heaven who tracks us, chases us, and then befriends us so we can joyfully choose to meet Him at the foot of the cross.

Chapter Five

We Do Not Tell the Truth to Other Christians Because We Are Uncomfortable in Confronting and Resolving Anger

ANGER IS A legitimate human emotion.

Since the first time we wailed because someone was not shoving that exquisite bottle of milk into our marauding mouth fast enough or the time the IRS informed us we owed them more of our hard-earned cash, we have become experts about experiencing and processing anger.

Anger is not polite or calculating. There is no time to be appropriately or thoughtfully angry. Instead it's a sudden eruption from a cauldron buried deeply within our psyche. Mark Twain wrote, "Anger is an acid that can do more harm to the vessel in which it is stored than to anything on which it is poured."[21] Twain knew anger could destroy not just a moment, but a life.

Scripture is laced with warnings about uncontrolled anger.

---

[21] Mark Twain, "Mark Twain Quotes," BrainyQuote, accessed October 20, 2017, https://www.brainyquote.com/quotes/quotes/m/marktwain120156.html.

The tragic story of the brothers, Cain and Abel, is precise about the damage of unbridled anger surrendered to its worst intent.

"...So Cain was very angry, and his face was downcast. The Lord said to Cain, 'Why are you angry? Why is your face downcast? If you do what is right, will you not be accepted? But if you do not do what is right, sin is crouching at your door...' While they were in the field, Cain attacked his brother Abel and killed him" (Gen. 4:5-8).

Anger is our primeval, knee-jerk response to any form of perceived victimization. If a driver on a rural two-lane highway passed the car in front of him and missed hitting your car by inches, wouldn't you experience anger? If your supervisor made negative comments about the quality and quantity of your work in front of coworkers, would you be angry? If a fellow believer in the Christian education class you taught stood and denigrated you with these words before the class concluded, "I suggest we totally change the content and the teaching methods used in this class...I am not getting much spiritual help here," would you be angry?

Have you ever threatened the driver of the car in front of you who obviously has never discovered the value of using a turn signal? Have you walked into your workplace staff meeting only to discover the meeting was cancelled, but no one thought this change was important enough to tell you? A bad day can be any twenty-four-hour period in which the clothes dryer decided not to work, the sky unloaded every ounce of water available onto your child's high school graduation ceremony, and the newspaper was thrown with precision, for the third time this week, into your front yard water fountain.

Whenever we are hurt, robbed, or threatened in any way, our reaction is to not-so-quietly nurture our boiling anger. Shakespeare penned this pithy point about anger in *The Taming of the Shrew*, "My tongue will tell the anger of my heart, or else my heart, concealing it, will break."[22]

Anger is not a pensive, silent emotion. Anger will not be kept waiting in the wings of our busy lives. It demands expression; it wants to jump on the nearest stage in the drama of our lives and scream, "I will not remain silent; these words are lies. I am furious that you would make a statement like this without any proof."

For people of faith, anger pockmarks Scripture. The Hebrew word for anger, *anaph* and the Greek *menis* both define the divine power of anger as "...dreadful, often fatal and should be feared and avoided at all costs."[23]

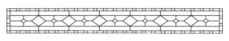

ANGER WILL NOT BE KEPT WAITING IN THE WINGS OF OUR BUSY LIVES. IT DEMANDS EXPRESSION.

Yahweh (God) seethed with anger on Mr. Sinai when Moses came down out of those dusty, ancient, rough rocks, and surveyed Israel's unbridled rebellion. Those divinely penned slate tablets defined Yahweh's rules for living. Anger smashed the sanctity of the words, the moment, and the place.

In Henry VI, Part Two, William Shakespeare captured the intensity of anger, as displayed on Mt. Sinai, when he wrote, "Could I come near your beauty with my nails, I could set my ten commandments in your face."[24]

Ouch!

---

[22] William Shakespeare, "The Taming of the Shrew," SCENE III. A room in PETRUCHIO'S house, accessed October 20, 2017, http://shakespeare.mit.edu/taming_shrew/taming_shrew.4.3.html.

[23] Patrick Considine, "The Theme of Divine Wrath in Ancient East Mediterranean Literature," SMEA Nuovo Serie, accessed October 20, 2017, http://smea.isma.cnr.it/wp-content/uploads/2015/07/Considine The-Theme-of-Divine-Wrath.pdf.

[24] William Shakespeare, "Henry IV, Part Two," SCENE III. The palace, accessed October 20, 2017, http://shakespeare.mit.edu/2henryvi/2henryvi.1.3.html.

Displays of anger are not pretty. We have all been the recipients, or owners, of out-of-control wrath. But anger also has assets.

Anger advises: "You are being violated right now...protect yourself." Sometimes, anger whispers, "Step out of this place and move away from this person right now. You need to use the anger you are feeling to aggressively identify and apply a solution to what is going on around you."

We must identify what was said or non-verbally acted out that created our response. Ask yourself, "Why am I feeling angry right now?" In biblical history, the disobedience of Adam and Even in the garden resulted in both being banished from their beautiful first home. God was angry because the covenant to which both He and the newlyweds had agreed, was broken in a matter of seconds in the middle of paradise.

Adam and all his descendants were sentenced to hard labor with no chance for parole. Yahweh was angry, and His fury resulted in changing the rules. He sent a catastrophic flood, destroyed Sodom and Gomorrah, and then sent plagues to afflict the landscape of Egypt.

Our first response to Adam and Eve's eviction may have been to scream at God, "What were You thinking? Cut these folks some slack. I mean, come on, they just moved in to their garden last week. Give them a break and how about a pinch of grace right now?"

What we learn from these pathetic patriarchs of our faith is that God, like us, is looking for a relationship steeped in integrity. What are the implications of this dusty trip into ancient history in light of our own fits of anger?

The first hard decision we must make when we tell the truth to fellow disciples of Christ is how will we resolve anger between each other.

Christians have five significant interpersonal skills you can employ when confronting anger anywhere in your life.

First, watch for the signs of anger and frustration in you. You will know you are quietly angry when: (1) you lose eye contact, (2) you grow increasingly quiet with someone with whom you are normally very verbal and emotionally frank, (3) you do not provide responses to questions that have been posed to you, (4) you frequently check the screen of your cell phone or scan the face of your wristwatch, and (5) leave a conversation without an explanation or excuse.

Second, if anger is undeniably present, verbally check your assumption with a question expressed like this, "I sense you do not agree with my account of what happened in the deacon's meeting last night. Tell me, am I correct or incorrect about my observations?"

When you feel angry, we normally leave quietly because the emotional baggage is too heavy to carry and process. This is avoidance.

The disadvantage of walking away from conflict is it can end a relationship. In the back of our minds we say to ourselves, "I cannot believe she still has a problem with me. Well, I am not playing this game." Physically and emotionally, we run into a protected silence, but the silence does not heal. Over time, silence can generate assumptions about each other not based in facts. Additionally, nothing has improved. The learned passive-aggressive behaviors employed by you and another believer only keep this non-productive relationship alive and well, if you want to call it that.

When we continue without hesitation to repeat non-productive behaviors, how can we ever expect a different outcome? With genuine intent, we can respond at this pivotal moment with an assertive statement like, "I am eager to resolve our differences and I am asking you to join me" instead.

Charlotte Bronte in her novel, *Villette*, said of the chief protagonist, "He fumed like a bottled storm."[25] The easiest choice is to personify the

---

[25] Charlotte Bronte, "Villette Quotes by Charlotte Bronte," Villette Quotes, accessed October 20, 2017, http://www.litquotes.com/quote_title_resp.php?TName=Villette.

"bottled storm" by walking around muttering to yourself, "Why can't people just do what they are supposed to do without ruining my life."

Can you hear that? It's the broken record of the victim. If we are comfortable in hitting the replay button on all our worst moments with someone, nothing will ever change. We will continue to project ourselves as the easy target, the victim, and the loser.

Third, look and listen for new options.

The my-way-or-the-highway attitude will destroy any friendship, marriage, or spiritual camaraderie. This emotional power play between people (who may share the same faith journey) will guarantee our tendency to regularly gulp down five pain relievers, three quarts of antacid or discover some elixir producing ten hours of a good night's sleep.

William Arthur Ward suggested, "It is wise to direct your anger towards problems—not people; to focus your energies on answers—not excuses."[26]

While serving as one of twelve chaplains at Harvard University for five years, I had the delight and challenge of meeting each week with eleven other clergy. Unfortunately, we often did not, because of our education, theology and doctrine... agree. What I learned from this group of colleagues, who became lifelong friends, was conflict did not have to divide us.

We took turns representing our different thoughts, education, and expressions of faith. Then we all agreed (even though each of us accepted the fact we were the only right and holy souls in the room) to listen to each other and actively explore our similarities.

You may want to use language like this when conflict comes out of the shadows: "Help me understand how your position will assist us so can we move forward. I may not agree, but I am convinced there is a larger

---

[26] William Arthur Ward, "William Arthur Ward Quotes," BrainyQuote, accessed October 20, 2017, https://www.brainyquote.com/quotes/quotes/w/williamart190448.h

issue here and it is unity." Mutually acceptable options are always a possibility, when conflict is verbally acknowledged. Distortion and unfounded assumptions will always fill silence. It is important you communicate clearly and approach each other humbly.

Fourth, we all bring our own unique psychological blocks to every conversation. We weave blocks into our most difficult conversations with our most difficult people.

The first blockage in resolving conflict is acknowledging words are permanent. Stop for a moment and answer this question, "What were the often-repeated words you heard from a parent or guardian when you were a child?" Did those words include, "Go to your room now and I will let you know when you can come out?"

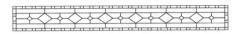

MUTUALLY ACCEPTABLE OPTIONS ARE ALWAYS A POSSIBILITY, WHEN CONFLICT IS VERBALLY ACKNOWLEDGED.

Or, "You are in big trouble…I am taking you to your grandmother's house and she will teach you a lesson or two." Or, "When I was a child, I never talked to my parents the way you are talking to me. Wait until your father comes home."

Words get superglued to our memories and emotions. The older we get, the better we are at digging into the canyons of our brains and unearthing both positive and negative words.

The second blockage we have when considering resolving conflict, especially with another believer, is quickly evaluating those who are standing in the shadows watching this conflict spin out of control. If we are honest, most of us want our audience to be in the wings, watching this verbal contest careen out of control. We carefully select both our words and tone of voice because we have people in the stands who are silently supporting us with a chant that goes something like this, "Two bits, four bits, six bits a dollar, all who are with our brother/sister, pray louder."

The liability of playing to the stands is we avoid addressing the real issues. When we are more concerned about appeasing the emotional and spiritual appetites of those watching from a distance, we will adopt positions and conclusions which we will often regret later.

The third blockage is an inability to put together a real sentence.

Here are three practical suggestions about words: (1) write them down, (2) read them out loud repeatedly in a private environment so you have gone over what you want to say, (3) commit your opening statement (one or two sentences) to memory. These steps will help you major on the majors and not get distracted.

You might also ask someone you trust to listen and critique your verbal approach and give you feedback. Remember, if you are trying to resolve conflict with someone you value, your choice of words is essential.

Verbal communication is enhanced when we stay with the subject-verb-object pattern. A clean sentence is structured like this: "I have a different perception of our conflict right now." "I" is the subject, "perception" is the verb and "our conflict" is the object.

The fourth blockage, and the church has excelled in its use, is name-dropping. It is not the name that is significant; it is when it is dropped. You know, "I was praying last night and the Lord God Almighty came and whispered 'hope' in my ear." I too am a person of faith and I am not questioning God's ability to be heard in our dreams, prayers, public worship or driving home after an exhausting day. His still small voice regularly booms into the silence of my sleep and my faith. Name-dropping has nothing to do with God, the Hound of Heaven, who regularly chases me down the alleyways of my life. Many times in my life, I am convinced, I heard His voice, but those divine whispers will always remain private.

The fifth and final blockage in our spiritual lives is our desire for a miracle. In the book, *Children*, by Catherine Pulsifer, the author wrote, "Look at the birth of a child, how can you not believe in miracles?"[27] When I leaf through the thousands of photos I have gathered through my life, I am overwhelmed by the predictable miracle of new life that has consistently decorated my life: Daphne and Niki, our daughters, introduced us to our grandchildren, over a span of fifteen years, to Nicholas, Zachary, Barrett and Liam. Our grandsons are without question the ultimate miracles in our lives.

Pivot back with me to the premise of this chapter. The presence and lifespan of anger also overwhelms us. We often strap on our well-worn, historic anger each day, hoping its biting presence will make us impervious to any hurt or new attacks that may be waiting for us tomorrow. If we only had a divine cure for this growing malignancy in our body, the lacerating pain in our emotions which regularly drips out acidic memories and disturbs our sound sleep, rendering it forever elusive.

We all need a miracle for our damaged memories and bodies. But we may have missed the advent of our miracle. We may have swallowed the miracle by allowing our habitual anger.

James may provide the conclusion to this chapter. *"Know this, my beloved brothers: let every person be quick to hear, slow to speak, slow to anger; for the anger of man does not produce the righteousness of God"* (James 1:19-20, ESV).

If we are frustrated with the lack of growth in our spiritual maturity, we may be mentally replaying scenes of difficult, angry conversations with other people of faith. The remedy, according to James, is time. But time does not heal all wounds, as many of us are led to believe. On the contrary,

---

[27] Catherine Pulsifer, "Inspirational Words of Wisdom," Miracle Quotes and Sayings, accessed October 20, 2017, http://www.wow4u.com/qmiracle/.

time can lance the words, the hurt, the violence, the rejection, and these quiet, but polluted, fountains can slowly fester forever.

We can protect our spirits and our minds by listening to James, and being "slow to speak" and "slow to anger." By slowing down our need to even the score, we open small windows for the power of God's Spirit to fill us with other options. Paul captured this ultimate, spiritual discipline when he penned, *"In your anger, do not sin: Do not let the sun go down while you are still angry"* (Eph. 4:26).

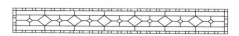

BY SLOWING DOWN OUR NEED TO EVEN THE SCORE, WE OPEN SMALL WINDOWS FOR THE POWER OF GOD'S SPIRIT TO FILL US WITH OTHER OPTIONS.

If you have found an inkling of hope in this chapter, it may be because anger is the silent killer you have intentionally hidden from yourself. Perhaps you have allowed anger a place in your heart.

We may not be telling each other the truth because anger is silently woven into the fabric of our spiritual relationships. Let's be honest, there is no reason to tell the truth when we are wallowing in our unspoken anger, or even rage.

We will tell each other the truth when we can say, through the love of our Lord, "I am, and have been, angry with you. I am asking for your time so I can explain why I am angry and then I want to hear your response. I know you will need time to think through my words and feelings. I am asking we provide each other with mutual respect as we talk and pray together and work this out."

CHAPTER SIX

WE DO NOT TELL THE TRUTH WHEN WE HESITATE TO DESCRIBE OUR RELATIONSHIP WITH GOD

HOW DO YOU experience God?

The answer to this question will have at least 800 billion answers. Throughout my pastoral ministry, I have asked parishioners to respond to this question and heard this: "God, for me, is like a close Friend who is a great listener," "God has been a thundering presence who normally only shows up in my worst moments," and "My view of God is a long-term Friend who can always be found in the early morning hours just before I stumble into my next, new hell."

Most Christians, from my experience, are uncomfortable describing their relationship with God, Jesus Christ, and the Holy Spirit.

I think I know why.

Have you ever been accosted by a religious zealot in the uncomfortable confines of an airport or worse in the plane ...for three hours? I have.

The minutes with this spiritual enthusiast dragged into a slow-motion theological discussion which had no beginning, and regretfully, no end. I listened and listened. I finally interrupted them and said, "I am a follower of Jesus Christ and I am committed and comfortable with my faith. I appreciate your zeal for your religious experience. Thank you for honoring my spiritual journey and my need to get back to reading and writing before we land."

If you have been the target of the over-zealous, religious type, you probably know the uncomfortable state of story. At the same time, people who have had a spiritual conversion experience know the freedom and future they gained from His exquisite good news. There is nothing else like it. One is forever changed.

John Wesley, in his *Journal,* wrote, "In the evening I went very unwillingly to a society in Aldersgate, where one was reading Luther's preface to the Epistle to the Romans. About a quarter before nine...I felt my heart strangely warmed. I felt I did trust Christ, Christ alone, for salvation; and an assurance was given me that He had taken away my sins, even mine, and saved me from the law of sin and death."[28]

Wesley's story is not mine, and may not be yours. But the clarity of his conversion is astounding and humbling.

We have all, at some place and time, stumbled into the tangible presence of God. We lost our ability to speak with the Creator, remaining quiet in the holiness of the moment. We could not physically move. Our brains screamed "Just stay silent. You are standing on holy ground." In this awe-inspiring moment when your heart, like Wesley's, was "strangely warmed," you knew you had been brushed by a divine wind.

There is a vast chasm between a committed follower of Jesus Christ and the many odd, but religious people in society today. There's the shallow on-again, off-again spiritual wanderer, looking for the next spiritual high. These spiritual junkies sit next to you, ready to recite 300 verses

---

[28] John Wesley, "Journal of John Wesley," Christian Classics Ethereal Library, accessed October 20, 2017, https://www.ccel.org/ccel/wesley/journal.vi.ii.xvi.html.

of Scripture by memory, or lean over a coffee shop counter and ask, "Could I have a few minutes of your time to tell you about Jesus Christ, the Lord of my life?" How about the knock on your front door at 9:00 a.m. on a Saturday morning which results in a ten-minute mini-sermon about the contrast between the pearly gates and the gates of hell? Then there's the driven zealot, continuously scouring an assortment of spiritual sites to find the next move of pure faith. And of course, there are those who jump around from church to church to church.

Some of these people can be unstable and dangerous. They are often marked by the following traits: They focus on any new, purer expression of faith and need to be part of a community built on a legalistic rule-oriented belief system. They are constantly dropping the name of someone

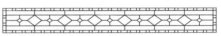

A DISCIPLE OF CHRIST IS A COMPASSIONATE BELIEVER WHO QUIETLY LOOKS FOR A NICHE TO BECOME THE HANDS, FEET AND HEART OF HIS LORD.

who has a position or who is a spiritual power in the spiritual community so they feel secure. They will also assert that prejudice is necessary to guarantee the purity of the group and are focused on maintaining a strict doctrinal reputation. Sadly, they may even resort to physical violence when they feel their community is threatened.

In contrast, a disciple of Christ is a compassionate believer who quietly looks for a niche to become the hands, feet and heart of his Lord. The Hebrew word for "follower" also means "learner." So if a follower of Jesus Christ wants to be a disciple, he needs to prepare his mind and emotions for the continuous advent of Christ-consciousness.

Christians are, therefore, constantly foraging through the mind of Christ. His followers are often ask, "What would Jesus do?" The answer to that question will drag us from passive religiosity to assertive discipleship. The assertive follower of Jesus Christ will possess a different set of characteristics.

First, there's boldness, a stream of boldness used to describe God's people in both the Old and New Testament.

"So do not fear, for I am with you; do not be dismayed, for I am your God. I will strengthen you and help you; I will uphold you with my righteous right hand" (Isa. 41:10).

Paul left us these words of encouragement, *"In him and through faith in him we may approach God with freedom and confidence* (boldness)" (Eph. 3:12, addition mine).

The psalmist was an isolated, smelly shepherd who had no designs on getting into the spiritual big leagues and then, *"When I called, you answered me; you greatly emboldened me"* (Psa. 138:3, underlining mine).

If I were advertising a full-day workshop, "How to Be Bold with Difficult People at Work," you might be interested in paying the $125.00 fee with coffee and donuts served at break times. God has called us, as His children, to be bold about communicating the vast expanse of His love and power. When we tell the truth, especially to fellow believers, we do not raise our voices, but we do, sometimes quietly and with resolute boldness, say, "Despite my failures and poor choices in life, Christ remains the Lord of my life and my yesterdays and tomorrows are all directed by His presence within me."

The early church experienced the power of Jesus, the Son of God. They were catapulted from fearfully hiding in the shadows to being the empowered messengers of the Messiah, *"After they prayed, the place where they were meeting was shaken. And they were all filled with the Holy Spirit and spoke the word of God boldly"* (Acts 4:31, underlining mine).

In our commodity-driven world, we have no inhibitions about turning to someone and asking, without any hesitation, "Where did you find that amazing purse? I just love the color and size. Do they have any more?" So why not ask the Creator of the universe to give us a relaxed freedom to boldly talk about the Hound of Heaven who tracked us and loved us enough to introduce us to Himself and eternity?

The second characteristic of the assertive Christian is someone who is committed to lifelong spiritual learning. Peter wrote, "*Therefore, with minds that are alert and fully sober, set your hope on the grace to be brought to you when Jesus Christ is revealed at his coming*" (1 Peter 1:13).

In a lifetime, we will only scratch the surface of understanding the depth, width, and height of God's love that was expressed in the agony of Christ's death on that solitary, cruel tree followed by the blessed emptiness of an Easter morning tomb.

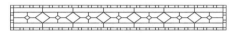

THE ASSERTIVE CHRISTIAN IS SOMEONE WHO IS COMMITTED TO LIFELONG SPIRITUAL LEARNING.

The third characteristic of assertive faith is a willingness to not just experience salvation but also speak about the joy and satisfaction of living as a child of God to the watching world around us.

The apostle Paul wrote in, "*For I am not ashamed of the gospel, because it is the power of God that brings salvation to everyone who believes...*" (Rom. 1:16a).

Do you hesitate about sharing your commitment to Christ openly because you do not want to be seen as a religious fanatic? Yes, a lifelong faith journey is a private decision. No one can make this decision for us, but is it not normal to tell others about an event or circumstance that literally saved your physical life? From surviving a skiing accident on the side of a mammoth, frozen mountain to hunkering down in a dank basement to escape the ravages of an approaching tornado, we aren't normally shy and quiet about talking about how we survived any kind of threat to our physical well-being.

Unfortunately, despite our experiences in the sweet presence of God, we often do not share the truth as God has revealed it to us in His Word and presence because we do not want to offend anyone and get labeled as one of those Christian wackos mentioned earlier. However, we are commanded in Scripture to share the Good News. Part of our job is to share our testimony of how we heard and responded to God with someone else.

The fourth characteristic of someone who has encountered Christ is his ability to capture and develop internal peace. The words of Christ, before His ascension, are a poignant reminder of our spiritual inheritance, *"Peace I leave with you; my peace I give you. I do not give to you as the world gives. Do not let your hearts be troubled and do not be afraid"* (John 14:27).

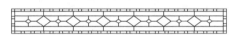

PART OF OUR JOB IS TO SHARE OUR TESTIMONY OF HOW WE HEARD AND RESPONDED TO GOD WITH SOMEONE ELSE.

In the middle of our sleepless nights and before there is a hint of a sunrise, we desperately search through our darkness and often find God. Whether it is a nation seeking silence on the battlefield or a distraught, sleepless parent waiting for the sound of a garage door going up at 1:00 a.m., we all pant for peace.

Bernard Baruch said, "Let us not deceive ourselves; we must elect world peace or world destruction."[29]

I seldom miss the annual Christmas Eve worship service. Even though my age is conspiring against my best intentions to slide into those wooden

---

[29] Bernard Baruch, "Bernard Baruch Quotes," BrainyQuote, accessed October 20, 2017, https://www.brainyquote.com/quotes/quotes/b/bernardbar169232.html.

pews at midnight, the peace and purity of those moments always urges me to come.

"Silent Night," "Oh Come, Oh Come, Emmanuel," and "Come Thou Long-Expected Jesus" grease the wheels of genuine spirituality for me. My soul is bathed in the quiet adoration of those flickering, candlelit moments. What do these four principles of an assertive faith have to do with "Why Christians Do Not Tell Each Other the Truth?"

We hesitate to initiate a conversation about our faith because we do not want to come across as the local spiritual guru. I have a lifetime of experience in parish ministry, plus not one, but two, theological degrees. But the truth is that none of us, regardless of our history, experience, or education, can lay claim to the title of "God's Expert about Everything."

Look around your community of faith. Are there people who stand out as quiet, powerful,

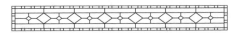

WE ARE DRIVEN TO OUR KNEES WHEN WE SCAN OUR SPIRITUAL SCRAPBOOKS AND PAGE THROUGH THE PROVEN HISTORY OF GOD'S PATIENT AND EVERLASTING LOVE.

peacemakers who are, indeed, spiritual giants? These are the Christians who have long histories in a particular worshipping community. We all want these spiritual leaders to verbally transport us to the good ol' days and embellish this trip down a spiritual memory lane with captivating stories, often embellished in holy and heavenly hyperbole.

The value of recounting our spiritual history is to dive, all over again, into the ocean of God's faithfulness to stay with us, speak to us, and correct us in our never-ending forays into faith. We are driven to our knees when we scan our spiritual scrapbooks and page through the proven history of God's patient and everlasting love.

We need to tell each other the truth. And the truth is that we have trudged through fast-moving rivers of pain, loneliness, despair, anger, and betrayal; and yet God, through the power of His Holy Spirit, has always whispered, *"Be strong and courageous. Do not be afraid or terrified because of them, for the Lord your God goes with you; he will never leave you nor forsake you"* (Deut. 31:6).

The best use of regularly scanning our individual spiritual history is to identify the attitudes, decisions, and failures that should not be duplicated in the future.

Have you heard about those inventions that never made it? There was the Flying Ford Pinto in 1970, which killed its inventors. And the Egg Cuber that cooked eggs placed in it and made them look like a Lego building block. And how about the Bell Rocket Belt which resulted in numerous injuries when its safety features failed and people fell from ten story buildings? Then there's the Joe Gilpin Motorized Surfboard, developed in 1940s, that never went faster than seven miles per hour. Oh, and the Baby Cage? Yes, you got it, it was a real cage put in a window.

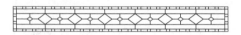

THE WORST MISTAKE ANY OF US COULD MAKE WOULD BE TO IGNORE OUR HISTORY.

Let's get personal. Get a clean sheet of notebook paper and make a list of all your worst decisions. When your list is complete, ask yourself, "What should I have boldly told myself or others when I knew this decision would never be the right choice?"

Sometimes we must tell ourselves the truth.

The worst mistake any of us could make would be to ignore our history. There will always be some wins but it is the losses we need to continuously review because life and faith are much easier when we remind ourselves what did not work or help.

Have you ever looked in a mirror and said, "Why did you think this would have been a wise choice? We have been down this road before." This discussion about repeating our worst personal and spiritual mistakes should lead us to faith.

The apostle Paul, someone I can identify with because he consistently failed too, gave us his honest appraisal of his inability to consistently do what he knew was right when he wrote, *"So I find this law at work: Although I want to do good, evil is right there with me. For in my inner being I delight in God's law; but I see another law at work in me...Who will rescue me from this body that is subject to death? Thanks be to God, who delivers me through Jesus Christ our Lord..."* (Rom. 7:21-25a).

This agonizing internal trouble, described in detail by Paul, is what telling the truth is all about. If you and I can openly and honestly talk to the person in our mirror, we have the potential for redemption. If we avoid this conversation, we also stuff our

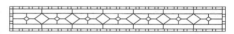

IF YOU CAN TELL THE TRUTH TO YOURSELF, YOU WILL FIND REDEMPTION.

ears with poor-me playdough and temporarily insulate ourselves from our worst fear we are all alone in this cold universe and... God is dead.

When you have finished reading this chapter, go to a private place with a writing pad and pen. Draw a straight line top to bottom of the blank sheet of paper. On the top of the left side write: *"My Worst Decisions"* and on the top of the right side write: *"The Reasons Why I Made These Worst Decisions."* This is a redemptive and private moment. If you can tell the truth to yourself, you will find redemption. If, on the other hand, you seldom take responsibility for your thoughts, behaviors and failures, you will not enjoy the delight of celebrating your humanity and the power of your faith.

Note that Paul never hesitated in declaring his relationship with God. There was no apologetic, "Oh, golly, gee whiz, I guess I just never thought anyone, especially God, could love me." Instead the apostle knew exactly who he belonged to and was not the least bit intimidated when confronted by an unbelieving world.

The prophet Nehemiah captured the essence of a righteous but forgiving God when he gave an overview and history of the Israelites with this description of his heritage and his God: *"But you are a forgiving God, gracious and compassionate, slow to anger and abounding in love..."* (Neh. 9:17b). When Nehemiah thought the other divine shoe would fall, God decided to dance around Israel to the joyous tune of His forgiveness.

Telling the truth will always require the truth-teller to stop playing religious and psychological games and be willing to face his mirror and say, "You knew this was the wrong decision. Stop whining and move on. Calling yourself names is not helping you."

As disciples of Christ, we have a lot to remember, and not all of it is good. Truth-telling begins with a multifaceted commitment to be bold enough to admit your failures, bold enough to stop blaming people and circumstances for your choices, and bold enough to say to anyone willing to listen, "I am imperfect, but loved and accepted by God."

CHAPTER SEVEN

WE DO NOT TELL THE TRUTH TO OTHER CHRISTIANS BECAUSE WE ARE UNCOMFORTABLE SAYING, "I DO NOT AGREE."

"AND, THEY WILL know we are Christians, by our love." This familiar worship song has wafted over pews, pulpits and prayer meetings for ages. It is laced with interpersonal warmth and acceptance regardless of differences in skin color, nationality, or IQ.

Christians, we have been taught, can be identified as brothers and sisters by their visual unity with each other. When Christians physically get together they will often show their emotional bond in hugs and warm, long-lasting handshakes.

Jesus, in the middle washing the feet of His disciples said, *"A new command I give you: Love one another. As I have loved you, so you must love one another. By this everyone will know that you are my disciples, if you love one another"* (John 13:34-35). The Messiah role-played The Sermon on the Mount when He washed the dirty, smelly feet of His followers and then stopped and knelt in front of Peter, who indignantly responded, *"No, you shall never wash my feet.' Jesus answered, 'Unless I wash you, you have no part of me'* (John 13:8).

In this tete-a-tete with the Son of God, the fledgling disciple, Peter, pulled back the curtain on the grandeur of salvation. The plan of redemption is simple: God calls us through the power and companionship of the Holy Spirit to hear this invitation, *"Come to me, all you who are weary and burdened, and I will give you rest"* (Matt. 11:28).

My father and mother were both ministers. The churches they pastored were small congregations, struggling to pay the utility bill and sometimes, the pastor's salary. There was no glitzy "Cathedral of Tomorrow" that dominated my spiritual history. The Sunday morning worship environment was often a cold, dank room decorated with immovable hard wooden pews. Despite the empty pews and offering plates, I learned a lot about the unfathomable abundance of God's grace in that small, often sparsely filled sanctuary.

As I grew in age and my faith, I discovered joy was not a transitory emotion that jumped on the stage of my life for about thirty seconds. Genuine joy was the result of God's peace and presence. Our Lord offered encouragement to His ragtag disciples before the Passover Feast with these words, *"Peace I leave with you; my peace I give to you. I do not give to you as the world gives. Do not let your hearts be troubled and do not be afraid"* (John 14:27).

Martin Luther said, "I have held many things in my hands, and have lost them all, but whatever I have placed in God's hands, that I still possess."[30] Luther was gifted by his Lord with supernatural peace that "passed

---

[30] Martin Luther, "Martin Luther Quote - God's Hands | ChristianQuotes.info," ChristianQuotes. info, December 16, 2013, accessed October 20, 2017, https://www.christianquotes.info/ images/martin-luther-quote-gods-hands/#axzz4w5hm33wP.

all understanding." In Luther's ominous days, when labeled a heretic—his ultimate protection was defined as divine peace.

We often shop around for a place of worship that will connect us with believers who share our perception of God. If one of these congregants becomes the "Weird Harold Believer" on our spiritual journey, we will either confront and correct this person, button our lip and smile, or leave.

And we will lose Luther's confidence: "…but whatever I have placed in God's hands, that I still possess." The statistics are not good about holding onto faith in a world that often mocks and belittles it. The number of people in America who call themselves Christian is dropping, according to a recent Pew Research Study. The number of Americans who identify with Christianity has also dropped drastically in the last eight years.

In Chapter 6, we discussed boldness. The characteristic cited in Scripture of those who became followers of Jesus Christ was boldness. When we come face-to-face with the faith of the early church, we also have to count those who actually sacrificed their breathing-in-breathing-out lives so more people would hear the good news. A martyr is somebody who suffers persecution and, ultimately, death for advocating and refusing to renounce a belief not in keeping with their spiritual truth.

I struggle to understand the faith and resolve of Polycarp, Stephen, Andrew, and Dietrich Bonhoeffer. These followers of Christ took their commitment to Him and His kingdom to an early grave. Others, like Amy Carmichael in India and Hudson Taylor in China, sacrificed their long lives to rescue the downtrodden and establish refuges for the needy in hostile cultures. They all left behind them a legacy of faith and service.

If our faith does not extend beyond attending a religious ceremony on Christmas, Easter and a few holy days, we may be struggling with fellow Christians in our community who discuss the cost of discipleship simply because we are not as we ought to be. Sometimes Christians do not tell each other the truth because we choose to be non-confrontational and shallow in our spirituality.

You may be asking, "What is wrong with the author of this book? Doesn't he know all Christians are really nice people? Rocking the religious boat only results in a 'holier-than-thou' nasty religiosity."

People who call themselves Christians are often reserved, intelligent and genuinely caring human beings. And if you look around your place of worship, regardless of the name over the front door, do you accept that no one in these pews is a perfect spiritual specimen? The answer is, inevitably,

WHEN GOD CALLS A MAN, HE BIDS HIM COME AND DIE."

yes. But we must remember the invitation of Christ has always been to "come and die." As Bonhoeffer was quoted earlier in this book: "When God calls a man, he bids him come and die."

This dying is not the stopping of the human heart. Rather, it is choosing to not speak ill of someone who is not in the room, not lie, not allow our anger and envy to run our lives, not live selfishly, and not exult in someone else's failure.

The question right now is, "If my place of worship is populated with one who told me he lied three times to his supervisor this past week, spoke ill of his coworker during the coffee break on Friday, and has no inhibitions about driving drunk, what does my faith tell me I need to include in my next conversation with him?"

This chapter is built on this assumption: People of faith can also, sometimes, over a period of time, be weak, faithless people. If the front doors of your church do not magically siphon off sinners, we all need to look at the final words of Jesus again. *Therefore go and make disciples of all nations, baptizing them in the name of the Father and of the Son and the Holy Spirit"* (Matt. 28:19).

Making disciples requires spiritual and interpersonal skills. We need to develop them.

The first skill will test your understanding of God. Another name for God in Scripture is the Great I Am. Notice the "I." There is a big difference in the meaning of a sentence when you use an "I statement" instead of a "you statement." One of the many ways you may serve your congregation is by preparing and administering the Lord's Supper each month. You have a reputation for timeliness and precision in making sure the elements, and those who are serving, have been prepared and any potential absence is known

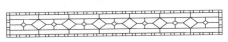

MAKING DISCIPLES REQUIRES SPIRITUAL AND INTERPERSONAL SKILLS.

well in advance. One of your normal servers did not show up for this past Sunday's communion worship and you were not notified ahead they could not participate. At the last minute, you found an alternate person to assist, but were dismayed the scheduled person had not had the courtesy to tell you about her absence.

Assuming you will contact this person, watch your choice of words. If you begin with, "You did not give me notice you would not be serving the Lord's Supper this past Sunday," the emotional atmosphere between the two of you will become confrontational. If this scenario happened, you could be prepared for waves of silence after those words followed by this response, "Well, I guess I disappointed you and the entire church. You can take me off the list for serving Communion in the future."

This confrontational moment could easily have been avoided if just one word had been changed at the beginning of this dialogue. Substitute "I" for "you" and listen to the change in the emotional atmosphere, "We should come up with a method so I will know when you will not be able to participate in the serving of the Lord's Supper. Do you have any suggestions?"

What is your emotional response when you hear, "You just do not understand what has been going on in my life this past week," or "I don't need you to criticize me"?

Listen for a significant shift in the other person if "I" is substituted for "you" in these same sentences: "I am eager to hear about the difficult issues in your life right now," and "I hear your frustration, and I want to know how I can be of help to you right now."

The second skill is to substitute a declaratory statement for a question. Let's respond with assertiveness to this negative statement: "This fund-raising program does not have a prayer of succeeding. No one will give to a new building program when our church is obviously in debt and not growing."

An alternative statement could be: "As we all know, our church has struggled growing in membership and finances. What creative ideas do any of us have to reverse this trend?" Open-ended questions are not confrontational. Questions provide the option to "play with ideas and suggestions" without judging if these ideas will work.

An additional, and visual, device which will create new ideas for difficult moments is called clustering. Let's assume you lead a group of lay people in a discussion about building an addition to the present church property. You may want to initiate the conversation by asking, "What are all the advantages of enlarging our campus to enhance our ministries?"

At this point in the process of birthing new ideas and approaches, finances are not considered. You can allay the fears of parishioners who believe you may be dabbling in crazy delusions by stating: "I can see some of you are concerned we cannot actually afford our dreams. Let me assure you, once we have created our future between our ears, and then on paper, we will then find realistic methods to fund our preferred future."

Direct the attention in the room to a flip chart, blackboard or PowerPoint presentation which will give you the option of placing this question in front of the group: "In order to add a new addition to our church campus, what would we have to do to convince the congregation this new building will provide additional opportunities to build the kingdom of God among us?"

After asking the question, draw a small circle in the middle. In the circle put a question like, "What has to change in our congregation for us to grow the kingdom of God among us?"

Undoubtedly, there will be a variety of responses. These responses can be captured with just a few abbreviated words, which are also placed in circles. Depending on the willingness of the participants to be creative, the number of circles will blossom.

When all the circles are in front of the group, the next question from the leader should be, "If we were to prioritize these ideas, which one would be first?" There will not be unanimity, but over a short period of time, a beginning point will emerge.

There is one final step when using the cluster method for brainstorming. Every circle in the cluster should be numbered in the order of its priority. This process may not be immediately complete because it takes time to accurately decide on the order of ideas, but eventually it will fall together. Of all the small circles, one probably reads "Number One." For example, if your church is in the beginning stage of planning a new addition to your worship center, looking at potential contractors may be one of the first numbers.

During this process, the naysayers will become apparent, but in this case, the negative folks in the room can be an asset. Their legitimate concerns about raising money, finding qualified builders, the emotional impact of the change on members, the present financial obligations, and anything else that comes up can be the perfect launching pad for alternative thinking. They will naturally help lay the foundation for healthy growth.

We do not tell each other the truth because we do not want to move out of comfortable, historic paradigms. Sometimes these patterns become long-term blockages to growth within the body of Christ. The statement, "We tried that before and it did not work," will pull the plug on any creative solution. The truth may not always be found in the past. What we may find in the past is just the normal.

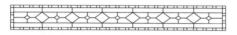

WE DO NOT TELL EACH OTHER THE TRUTH BECAUSE WE DO NOT WANT TO MOVE OUT OF COMFORTABLE, HISTORIC PARADIGMS.

The normal can include, "Let's not rock the boat in our church." When no leaves the past, the future remains elusive. You see, the truth is often determined by the level of safety people feel in any endeavor. Unfortunately, the safety of the normal can mire us in the quicksand of a slow, painful decline.

Have you been part of a part of the body of Christ that slowly ground into oblivion? After a while, fewer people attended, the cushioned maroon bottom of the offering plate became easier to see, and finding a parking place became easier with each passing Sunday. The church, like any organization, can slip into an ambiguous future when its mission is obscured, destined to disintegrate into its own organizational dust.

If you have traveled around the world, you probably have stepped into magnificent cathedrals that no longer have a congregation. Aside from the tourist buses that pull up to these magnificent ancient doors, there is not a sniff of spiritual life.

When we tell the truth to each other in the body of Christ, we will move past who we are in our worst moments, and fall into the grandeur of God's expansive power.

The author of Hebrews knew this truth. The sacrificial offering of the flesh and blood of God's Son sweltered in our dust and then saved us. In Hebrews, we hear these resounding and assuring words: *"Jesus Christ is the same yesterday and today and forever"* (Heb. 13:8).

The final expression of God's truth is our willingness to say no to false faith. Have you noticed it is getting harder to find the real thing? The diamond glistening on your finger may be a moissanite. A white sapphire in your jewelry drawer could be a crystalline form of aluminum oxide called corundum. And a cubic zirconia, a less expensive alternative to a natural diamond, is called a diamond simulant now.

Faux is in. What are the implications for our faith in a world where it is difficult to find an original?

It begins and ends with saying no.

Christians cannot tell the truth to each other, or our watching world, if we continually water down the wonder of being called a child of God. First, the church has to decide to tell the truth about the impact of our technology on the truth. We all have gadgets. I love my Apple Mac. My iPhone is a constant, highly protected object attached to my body at any given time.

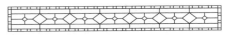

CHRISTIANS CANNOT TELL THE TRUTH TO EACH OTHER, OR OUR WATCHING WORLD, IF WE CONTINUALLY WATER DOWN THE WONDER OF BEING CALLED A CHILD OF GOD.

And the iPad that slips so smoothly into my briefcase is my window to the world. Never in my lifetime have I ever felt this connected.

But at what cost? Spiritual boldness is essential as our gadgets become our gods. We should be asking these questions of each other as we boot up for another day of navigating the bites and bits: Can we turn off our technology and still be at intellectual and emotional ease with each other in the body of Christ? How much time is too much time to spend with an inanimate object that does not breathe in and out like me? Does this thin, metallic device have the right to direct my next conversation and my future next week?

Second, the truth has to include "I do not agree." In my teenage years, I was taught the mark of a true Christian was someone who could boldly say no to all the enjoyable things in life. The list of the enjoyables got longer every day. The list included sneaking into a movie theatre, smoking a cigarette, using a curse word I heard in my junior high locker room, dancing—even in the privacy of my bedroom, and thinking thoughts that usually had something to do with sex. The list went on and on.

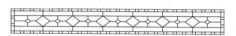

THE ONE PERSON WE PROBABLY STRUGGLE NOT AGREEING WITH IS OUR SELF.

It has taken a lifetime for me to acknowledge to myself that avoiding some of the vices on these lists probably spared me physical and emotional harm. At the same time, I have learned I needed to tell myself the truth too. I should have said, "I do not agree."

The one person we probably struggle not agreeing with is our self. In the past ten years, I have learned being honest with yourself is a daunting challenge. For most of my life I blamed and avoided the deficiencies I found in my mirror. My distress was usually the result of telling myself there was someone else, not me, invading my world with pain and problems.

As I have become honest with myself, I also got honest with my Lord. In the past few years I have folded my failures tightly around my psyche and my faith. I have surrendered and willingly owned the good of my successes and equally owned the agony of my failures. The first person I needed to get comfortable confronting with "I don't agree" was me.

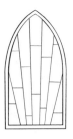

Chapter Eight

We Do Not Tell the Truth to Other Christians Because the Truth Can Damage a Long-Term Friendship

C.S. Lewis wrote, "Friendship is born at the moment when one person says to another: 'What! You too? I thought I was the only one.'"[31]

A lifelong friend is a gift that can be unwrapped and enjoyed every day because, as long as the two of you regularly communicate, irritate each other together, laugh together, disagree together and are comfortable just being silent in the same space...together, the result will be an undefinable and unbreakable, human bond.

Johnny Dowd, Bobby Dixon, Betty Ann Herzog, Daryll Merkel, Gary Eisenhower, Barb Gaylor, George Wood and Claudia Hartner are just a sampling of the names that have decorated my life with their lifelong commitment to be my friends.

People who are faithful friends decorate our days with delight and devotion. These people are often quiet, protected treasures imbedded in

---

[31] C. S. Lewis, "Values.com," Values.com, accessed October 20, 2017, https://www.values.com/inspirational-quotes/7434-friendship-is-born-at-that-moment-when-one.

the bedrock of our identity. The term best friend also belies the undeniable fact that we have acquired hordes of friends during our journey through the boxes on our calendar. Some of these people call us by first name when we walk into their workplace. Others silently nod and then smile. And, then there are the friends, we have not seen in years, but could "pick up where we were" in a nanosecond. Our closest friends are identified by their commitment to always remember our birthdays and anniversaries with an expensive Hallmark card or bouquets of flowers. Still others can predict our words when we serve up a genuine surprise. You know, "Oh, you should not have spent all this money...to remind me I am another day older."

I recently heard this definition of a best friend: "A friend is someone who knows the song in your heart and can sing it back to you when you have forgotten the words."[32]

Who are the singers in our lives? You know, the people who decorate our days with devotion and dancing. They are the ones that risk being misunderstood to say what we may not want to hear.

Even our literature is littered with the warmth of friends: Hamlet and Horatio, Tom Sawyer and Huck Finn, and the hilarious chemistry of Sancho Panza and Don Quixote. We have all been sucked into the vortex of these literary friendships. After we have been treated to an emotional, sometimes ancient story, we often begin tapping a series of numbers on our phones so we can hear the comforting voice of a special someone.

Good friends are hard to find and more difficult to keep.

There is a sign I have kept on my desk for years. It reads: "Never forget three types of people in your life: (1) the people who helped you through difficult times, (2) the people who left you in difficult times, and (3) the people who put you in difficult times."

---

[32] "Friendship/Friend Quotes and Proverbs," Classic HeartQuotes Archive, accessed October 20, 2017, http://heartquotes.com/Friendship.html.

This anonymous sign has the potential to result in both smiles and tears. The tears are an emotional claxon warning there is an impending loss. At that moment, you will suddenly know the meaning of victimization. Nothing hurts like the betrayal and loss of a friend. A friendship is a relationship built, probably for years, on a foundation of trust. You feathered the nest of a strong friendship with words of worth and hours of happiness only to watch, in horror, as the sanctity of your trust was torn apart by someone, you are convinced, you never knew.

Betrayal is not always delivered with words. Sometimes silence delivers the bad news, and that silence is worse than screaming. Our emotions would much prefer hearing a litany of acidic words instead of wandering through a wasteland of silence.

For the Christian, the death of a friendship can be catastrophic because mutual trust, patience and honor are embedded in our common theology about God. Disciples of Jesus Christ will often describe a meaningful friendship as a gift from God. Throughout my pastoral ministry, I have listened to heartbroken people mourn the absence of a lost friend. The yawning empty hole in their lives

FOR THE CHRISTIAN, THE DEATH OF A FRIENDSHIP CAN BE CATASTROPHIC BECAUSE MUTUAL TRUST, PATIENCE AND HONOR ARE EMBEDDED IN OUR COMMON THEOLOGY ABOUT GOD.

never seemed to be filled again with the passage of time. This hole in their hearts remain tender and never seemed to completely heal.

When we dab our damage with the ointment of time, we often build layers of scar tissue which sometimes makes it possible to repair our devastated hearts and promises. Scripture contains profound words of comfort for people of faith who have been deeply scarred by the betrayal of a friend.

"The Lord is close to the brokenhearted and saves those who are crushed in spirit" (Psa. 34:18).

"He heals the brokenhearted and binds up their wounds" (Psa. 147:3).

"Come to me, all of you who are tired from carrying heavy loads, and I will give you rest. Take my yoke and put it on you, and learn from me, because I am gentle and humble in spirit; and you will find rest. For the yoke I will give you is easy, and the load I will put on you is light" (Matt. 11:28-30, GNT).

The initiative of God to heal and restore those of us who have been damaged by the words and decisions of others is not in question. In the words of the hymn, "And Can It Be That I Should Gain?" we discover the restorative power of His grace: "And can it be that I should gain an interest in the Savior's blood? Died He for me, who caused His pain? For me, who Him to death pursued? Amazing love. How can it be that Thou, my God, shouldst die for me?"

This continuous whisper of God's unmerited grace infuses us with the possibility that the damage we suffered in a broken long-term relationship can be healed and even restored. What keeps us going and growing are the words we just read from Matthew 11: *"Come to me, all of you who are tired from carrying heavy loads, and I will give you rest. Take my yoke and put it on you and learn from me, because I am gentle and humble in spirit; and you will find rest."*

Finding "rest" is an apt transition to the fundamental assumption of this chapter: "...the Truth Can Damage a Long-term Friendship."

To find a friend for life can be a daunting task. The unexpected changes of human emotions, thoughts and actions will often challenge, and even sever, the bonds of friendship. Emotional pain can remain for a lifetime when you have heard these words from someone who you invited into the inner sanctum of your life, "I thought you were a friend I could trust. I guess I was wrong."

The internal devastation of these words may dissipate somewhat with the passage of time, but emotionally harmful words from someone we trusted have the potential to resurrect themselves into a haunting haze when we're searching for sleep. The truth is we will weep and agonize as we page through the memories of our lost and damaged friendships.

Sheryl Condie wrote, "A friend is someone you can be alone with and have nothing to do and not be able to think of anything to say and still be comfortable in the silence."[33] Condie's definition agrees with Scripture.

Christ crafted a definition for nurturing friendships. He said, "*My command is this: Love each other as I have loved you. Greater love has no one than this: to lay down one's life for one's friends. You are my friends if you do what I command. I no longer call you servants, because a servant does not know his master's business. Instead, I have called you friends, for everything that I learned from my Father I have made known to you*" (John 12:12-15).

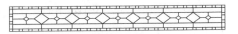

A FRIEND MOVES INTO THIS POSITION BECAUSE THE RELATIONSHIP IS BUILT ON AN EMOTIONAL CONNECTION, NOT PERFORMANCE.

There are three qualities of friendship in the words of Jesus.

First, friendship is not legal or compulsory. Second, friendship is directly linked to our ability to experience and communicate love. Third,

---

[33] Rhea Ghosh, "Sheryl Condie on Friendship," Friendship and leaving, accessed October 20, 2017, https://www.mtholyoke.edu/~rghosh/index/quotes/friendship.html.

the difference between servant and friend is a distinction which is hard to avoid. A friend moves into this position because the relationship is built on an emotional connection, not performance. Performance is the measure of a servant, not a friend.

A genuine friend is someone who, regardless of distance or how long it has been since the last phone call, will sneak into our memory bank and joyfully leave their footprints all over our psyche and emotions. An anonymous writer penned this definition of a friend, "Friendship isn't about who you've known the longest. It's about who walked into your life and said, 'I'm here for you, and then proved it.'"

This five-tissue definition of friendship opens our minds and souls to understand the generosity of God's grace which showed itself most starkly on Golgotha's hill. When we have been chased by the Hound of Heaven and cornered by His boundary-less love, we know the bliss of finally being accepted by God, regardless of our failures, rebellion and egocentricity.

Therefore, I can gain an interest in my Savior's love. Humming in the background, we should practice the following six spiritual disciplines when telling the truth to a friend.

First, each of us, regardless of our spiritual credentials, always has the choice to malign or intentionally misrepresent a fellow Christian. As disciples of Jesus Christ, here is another option.

President Dwight D. Eisenhower wrote that "if a man's associates find him guilty of phoniness, if they find that he lacks forthright integrity, he will fail. His teachings and actions must square with each other."[34] The first great need, therefore, is integrity and high purpose.

---

[34] Christopher Menuey, "The 3 'C's of Leadership," Air Force Global Strike Command, March 15, 2013, accessed October 20, 2017, http://www.afgsc.af.mil/News/Commentaries/Display/Article/455498/the-3-cs-of-leadership/.

The idea that someone's "teachings and actions must square with each other" open possibilities in a fractured relationship. If we cannot tell each other the truth because we are convinced the truth will make the other person unhappy, then we have a fake friendship which will eventually implode.

Scripture has many simple instructions about how to confront another believer who does not share our perceptions. Paul wrote, *"Therefore each of you must put off falsehood and speak truthfully to his neighbor, for we are members of one body"* (Eph. 4:25).

Here are four, consecutive verbal statements to use when telling the truth to another person, especially if this individual is a person of faith:

(1) "I would like a few moments of your time to respond to our conversation yesterday."

(2) "I did not agree with your conclusion and I would appreciate a few minutes of your time to tell you what I was thinking and feeling."

(3) "I want to hear your thoughts and feelings in return."

(4) "Thank you for your honesty and even though we obviously do not agree, I am committed to our friendship and our mutual faith."

We can also request the involvement of a third party. Sometimes neither you nor the other believer have the spiritual, emotional, and verbal skills to work through a serious disagreement. Telling the truth can create emotional and spiritual dissonance. Sometimes neither you nor the other party will do a good job figuring out the belief systems that are on the line

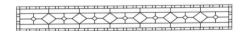

SOMETIMES NEITHER YOU NOR THE OTHER PARTY WILL DO A GOOD JOB FIGURING OUT THE BELIEF SYSTEMS THAT ARE ON THE LINE BETWEEN YOU; AND AN IMPARTIAL THIRD PARTY MAY BE ABLE TO HELP YOU BUILD NEW BRIDGES AND MEND THOSE FENCES.

between you; and an impartial third party may be able to help you build new bridges and mend those fences. If this option is of interest to you, be prepared to: (a) accept constructive criticism from that third party, (b) be open to a different approach in order to solve the misunderstanding, (c) improve your interpersonal communication skills, (d) learn how to compromise, and (e) hear a solution that may not be acceptable to either party.

Jeremiah is excruciatingly honest about our humanity: *"Everyone deceives his neighbor, and no one speaks the truth; they have taught their tongue to speak lies; they weary themselves committing iniquity"* (Jer. 9:5, ESV).

The easy choice is to always vote for yourself. When we proclaim, "I am my own savior," the options for divine intervention become limited. We may, when no one else is in earshot, look in our full-length mirror and boldly declare, "You are not perfect, but you are a person of integrity and honesty. Your Lord will walk with you into this difficult conversation."

Like I suggested in the previous chapter, draw a straight line down the center of clean sheet of paper. This time, at the top of the left-hand side, write: "My Assets." At the top of the right side, write: "My Liabilities." These assets and liabilities can be in any area of your life (vocation, family responsibilities, financial stability, spirituality, relaxation, whatever). List them.

When you are finished with both these lists, answer these questions: Which side of the paper was easier to compose? As an individual, are you more positive or negative? What item have you listed on either side that you know you need to change or improve?

This short exercise should produce joy and concern. The joy is in knowing you are genuinely a gifted person who has much value to share with people. The pain is you may have become one-dimensional, possibly an upsetting term.

If you are comfortable in just your skin and your opinions, and you have no interest or desire to accommodate people who do not match your style for worship, work and wisdom, you will become an isolated and possibly an angry person. When you always have to be right you limit your humanity and spirituality. Saying, "You know what, I was wrong" can be the most liberating moment of your life because you told the truth.

You know the truth. Right? If you have successfully maneuvered through puberty, have a credit card with a zero balance and are able to pay a mortgage payment every month, you are living the American dream. Is this the truth though?

Singer Peggy Lee penned these words in her hit song, "Is That All There Is":

"Is that all there is, is that all there is
If that's all there is my friends, then let's keep dancing
Let's break out the booze and have a ball
If that's all there is."[35]

For people of faith, the "booze and having a ball" may not be the problem. The real spiritual challenge for a Christian today is moving out of a spiritual mindset in which they only speak to other ones of the elect; these conversations are about how good we are and how decadent the rest of world is, and why these folks are on a fast train to hell.

THE REAL SPIRITUAL CHAL-
LENGE FOR A CHRISTIAN
TODAY IS MOVING OUT OF A
SPIRITUAL MINDSET IN WHICH
THEY ONLY SPEAK TO OTHER
ONES OF THE ELECT.

---

[35] Mike Stoller, "Is That All There Is?" by Jerry Leiber, recorded August 1969, in Is That All There Is? Peggy Lee, Capitol, 1969, vinyl recording.

Spiritual elitism is the worst liability of the church. There is no good news coming from Christians who are breaking their arms, patting each other on the back as they smile with satisfaction they are safe in the arms of God.

Fundamentally, there are only two options for the disciple of Jesus Christ: Make excuses for their weak and lifeless faith or own the cost of discipleship. Dietrich Bonhoeffer wrote, "Salvation is free, but discipleship will cost you your life."[36] And Bonhoeffer lived and died by his words.

There is no cost for our lives if we are one-dimensional and pompously believe we know all we need to know about God. You know, when we do not want to talk about our faith because it is a personal decision, or when we indulge fellow believers with, "Well, there are a lot of ways to find God."

If you remember an earlier quote, Bonhoeffer's "cheap grace" was soaked in these profound words, "When Christ calls a man, He bids him come and die."[37]

Cheap grace was the ground floor of Bonhoeffer's faith. He wrote:

"Cheap grace means grace as a doctrine, a principle, a system...Cheap grace is the preaching of forgiveness without repentance, baptism without church discipline, Communion without confession...Cheap grace is grace without discipleship, without the cross, grace without Jesus Christ, living and incarnate."[38]

So, what does this radical invitation to share in the death of our Lord mean in regard to our fear of telling each other the truth, especially a good friend?

---

[36] Dietrich Bonhoeffer, *The Cost of Discipleship* (New York: Simon and Shuster, 1995).

[37] Ibid.

[38] Ibid.

The core principle of a committed Christian is summed up in this hymn: "My hope is built on nothing less than Jesus' blood and His righteousness. I dare not trust the sweetest frame but wholly lean on Jesus Name. On Christ the solid rock I stand, all other ground is sinking sand."[39]

Those hyper-spiritual people we discussed earlier scare me. Have you been accosted on a street corner by someone waving a Bible in your face? Were you ever told you were going to hell unless you repented right now?

The best evangelism does not include assaulting unbelievers with their sins and mistakes. Christians draw people to their Savior when they recount His grace and mercy. His love and grace always wins.

If grace greases the skids for all of us to slide into the kingdom of God, how do we tell the truth to someone we value, especially a close friend?

We begin by boldly defining the ground floor of this relationship. The words may include, "We have known each other for eighteen years and shared both laughter and tears. We have not always agreed with each other, but we have a bond that has always held us together."

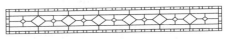

CHRISTIANS DRAW PEOPLE TO THEIR SAVIOR WHEN THEY RECOUNT HIS GRACE AND MERCY.

Reviewing the history between the two of you, good and bad, is a positive way to begin this conversation. Your next words could be, "I need you to tell me if I am right or wrong, but I sense you do not agree with the position I have taken at our church about spending less money on adding additional administrative staff instead of putting aside more resources for an evangelistic outreach to our community. What is your response to my observation?"

---

[39] Edward Mote, "The Solid Rock," *Timeless Truths Free Online Library*, accessed October 21, 2017, http://library.timelesstruths.org/music/The_Solid_Rock/.

Wait until the other person has clearly shared his/her thoughts and feelings and don't interrupt them. If you interrupt, you will hurt the relationship.

Next, look for the areas in which the two of you can agree. Highlight how much you appreciate this person's honesty, even though you may have a different opinion or perception. Affirming honesty does not mean you are endorsing what you have just heard.

Finally, summarize how the two of you can move forward. This stage includes providing due dates and a clear description of the communication channels each of you can expect. Allow for more time for each of you to add additional comments.

Do all conversations like this need to end in prayer? Yes! When Christ, the Lord of both of your lives, is invited to be part of our shared futures, hope has a chance. Allow the Holy Spirit to touch you both. Submitting to Him in prayer allows God, through the power of His Holy Spirit, more time to speak to us, and give us creative solutions. Sometimes He introduces solutions no one could ever have imagined.

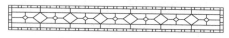

AFFIRMING HONESTY DOES NOT MEAN YOU ARE ENDORSING WHAT YOU HAVE JUST HEARD.

When we work at understanding what shared faith means in practice we savor the Savior's work in healing and then sealing long-term, faith-centered friendships.

CHAPTER NINE

WE DO NOT TELL THE TRUTH TO OTHER CHRISTIANS BECAUSE THE TRUTH WILL FORCE US TO LOOK IN OUR OWN MIRROR

AT THE HEART of this chapter is the assumption that God, because of His continuous promise to love and accept us, will fold His everlasting arms around us in eternity, and whisper, "Welcome home, you good and faithful servant."

It's a spiritual slam-dunk. Right?

In *The Problem of Pain* by C.S. Lewis, the author puts into words what most of us have considered, but probably not resolved: "That the lost soul is eternally fixed in its diabolical attitude we cannot doubt: but whether this eternal fixity implies endless duration—or duration at all— we cannot say."[40]

Lewis' second-guessing slips easily into the spiritual agenda of any Christian. If you have lived long enough, prayed long enough, given money to the church long enough and silently wondered if God can be trusted

---

[40] Clive S. Lewis, *The Problem of Pain* (New York, NY: HarperCollins, 2014).

with your eternity long enough, you have something in common with Lewis, Karl Barth, Hans Kung, Marilynne Robinson and N.T. Wright—all of whom have wrestled with the absolute truthfulness of God's promises.

We are continually reminded and intimidated by our habitual sin, which likes to hit the replay button and often cause sleepless nights. This process in which our worst mistakes and failures are replayed over and over again, leaves us exhausted and threatens our walk with God.

Paul's words are a poignant reminder of our inability to maintain purity of thoughts and deeds. He wrote, *"For I do not do the good I want to do, but the evil I do not want to do — this I keep doing. Now if I do what I do not want to do, it is no longer I who do it, but it is sin living in me that does it"* (Rom. 7:19-20).

Some of us, right now, are giving high-fives to the apostle Paul who was so transparent with God...just like the rest of us who desperately scream for divine help in this eternal battle with sin.

When we came face-to-face with God, through the life and resurrection of His Son, we joyfully surrendered our future to the King of Kings and the Lord of Lords. The euphoria of knowing our life and eternity were already paid for by a dark, dank empty tomb filled us with laughter, joy and the hope of a future without...an end.

But tomorrow can morph into just another day. The routine of the hot shower, finding clean clothes that match, munching an energy bar while navigating through a labyrinth of distracted drivers, trying to concentrate on the latest CNN radio update, lugging a bulging briefcase to a desk too small for another big day, heading for the fourth cup of java... and the familiar ends in fatigue as we drag ourselves home.

We have all met Walter Mitty. He makes an appearance every morning and night in our bathroom mirror. The come-day-go-day cadence of our pulsating lives beat out the same, numbing familiar tone we hear every morning. We like change, but repeating yesterday continues to have an arresting appeal.

Admitting this reality, let's go back to the words of the Apostle Paul, *"For I do not do the good I want to do, but the evil I do not want to do — this I keep doing"* (Rom. 7:19).

Like riding the same merry-go-round for hours and even days, we maneuver through life realizing that, "Wait a minute, we have seen this movie before." It is like a scene out of the *Groundhog Day.*

This is Paul's message to the young believers in Rome, and to those of us who are still trying to figure out their faith. Even though our salvation is assured, our theology intact, and we have memorized the Sermon on the Mount, we are all newbies, wandering around on the ground floor of God's grace.

Paul also captured our limitations *and* our limitless future with these words, *"For now we see only a reflection as in a mirror; then we shall see face to face. Now I know in part; then I shall know fully, even as I am fully known"* (1 Cor. 13:12).

We cannot get mired in the future. In spite of the pearly gates ahead of us, we have to get up every day and trudge through our trials and terror. When we get up to our kneecaps in slowly rotting relationships, dead-end careers, and empty bank accounts, we realize we have, as redeemed children of God, difficult choices to make.

Here is where the truth makes a cameo appearance. The indisputable truth about dealing with the truth is our best intentions, wishes, and hopes do not alter the truth.

Sometimes the truth is a marriage is cold and distant. Or that you do not make enough money to match the unpaid bills at the end of each month. If you believe God is dead, that is your truth. But it is not *the* truth.

We cannot understand the reality of God Almighty who chases us with love and acceptance.

If we do not tell other Christians the truth because the truth will force us to look in our own mirror, we have to, literally, have a "come-to-Jesus" moment with...our self.

I would much rather verbally take on my worst enemy than deal with the person in my mirror. I may be able to schmooze my clients, family or an IRS representative, but I will stammer and go silent when I know I am guilty as sin when I stare in my mirror. This confession drags us to our knees, followed by honest conversations with God. And although this is painful at first, what a relief it is in the end.

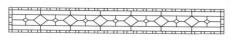

IF WE DO NOT TELL OTHER CHRISTIANS THE TRUTH BECAUSE THE TRUTH WILL FORCE US TO LOOK IN OUR OWN MIRROR, WE HAVE TO, LITERALLY, HAVE A "COME-TO-JESUS" MOMENT WITH...OUR SELF.

When talking with the Almighty, the easiest approach is pull out a verbal whip and wince through some serious self-truths. It is easier to slide into a poor-me rant with the person in my mirror than to tell God the truth.

Many people find it easier to feel badly about themselves than to choose to make changes. Making the decision to hug the pain and deal with its source is difficult. It is so much easier to wear the "I have been wearing the Loser Award all my life," than it is to admit it is time to change.

William Saroyan wrote, "Good people are good because they have come to wisdom through failure. We get very little wisdom from success."[41]

---

[41] William Saroyan, "William Saroyan Quotes," William Saroyan - Wikiquote, accessed October 23, 2017, https://en.wikiquote.org/wiki/William_Saroyan.

Picture another believer standing in front of you. You have just told them the complete truth about yourself, leaving nothing out. Can you imagine how intimidated you might feel around them now?

Intimidation is the result of instantaneously paging through your own history and confessing to yourself that you have failed, big-time. Telling the truth begins with hugging the hurt of owning our worst moments and our worst words. Without excuse, we need to admit we are guilty as charged.

Our histories are littered with the stinking, quiet carrion of promises to ourselves we have intentionally not kept. And our worst choice, assuming the previous paragraph is true, is to emotionally and spiritually throw another pity party over the truth of our sad state. This is the predictable moment when we complain to God, "I am worthless and despicable, and You know it. I live with this pathetic truth every day when I look in the mirror."

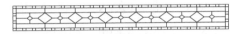

THE CALL OF CHRIST IS FOR THE *"WEARY AND BURDENED"* TO QUIETLY NESTLE INTO HIS QUIET PRESENCE AND ALLOW HIS *"REST"* TO REJUVENATE OUR INTIMIDATED SOULS.

Although this may have the appearance of truth, this rant is the easy way out. We have another choice.

Scripture defines this option with these instructions, *"Come to me, all you who are weary and burdened and learn from me, for I am gentle and humble in heart, and you will find rest for your souls"* (Matt. 11:28-29).

There is no magic elixir for the pain we experience when staring our sin in the face. The call of Christ is for the *"weary and burdened"* to quietly nestle into His quiet presence and allow His *"rest"* to rejuvenate our intimidated souls.

The next stage of redemption, when initiating a conversation with our mirror, is to be honest about the health of our self-esteem. Self-esteem has everything to do with how much value we ascribe to ourselves. A working definition of self-esteem can include having confidence in one's worth or abilities and developing internal self-respect as a response.

Effective self-esteem is when we have undeniably failed and can still look in the mirror and say, "You are not perfect and you proved that today to everyone in that conference room. What did you learn you need to change in the future when a similar situation arises?"

The easiest response is to beat yourself up, thinking, "Why do I always screw up at the worst times? I just need to shut my mouth and keep my thoughts and opinions to myself. I am a weak person who will not amount to much." This attitude is what I call the Eeyore Syndrome.

You may have met Eeyore if you ever heard the timeless children's tale, *The House at Pooh Corner* by A. A. Milne. Eeyore is a dejected and damaged stuffed donkey. And Eeyore has a poor opinion of most of the other animals in his neighborhood, describing them thus, "They haven't got Brains, any of them, only grey fluff that's blown into their heads by mistake..."[42]

This fanciful character will make you laugh, then cry. Eeyore just cannot see or accept his own limitations. He bumbles around this children's tale, constantly reminding people how put upon and flawed he is.

The Eeyore Syndrome (my creation), is often found in mature adults who delight in reminding everyone how much their world is set up to hurt and abuse them. Sometimes Christians slide into the Eeyore Syndrome. They have crafted a whining persona that excels in being self-absorbed. They are mired in their own failure, but somehow never responsible for their own moping.

---

[42] A. A. Milne, *The House at Pooh Corner* (New York: E. P. Dutton, 1956), 13.

In my forty years of experience I have found there are people in the church who get satisfaction in being agents of change, but not necessarily changes for the better. What do they get out of polluting the parish? It is all about the power of influence. When any person, nestled comfortably into a collection of other flawed people, creates havoc, they can experience a smug sense of silent satisfaction. They also tend to develop a following of other slightly disgruntled people. The power of this kind of moment can become addictive. Their goal becomes exerting their influence for the sake of doing it. However, the churchgoer who is adept at

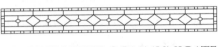

USE SILENCE TO COMMUNICATE

stirring the parish pot has nothing to show for it at all, if the result of this sacred stew is negative, divisive, and alienating.

How do you respond to this self-absorbed saint? You tell the truth.

Here are some sequential interventions you can use with the difficult person in your church.

First, ask for a meeting with this fellow believer in a private, neutral place. Do not get together at either home. Personal space will prejudice the conversation.

A potential opening statement for this meeting could be: "I appreciate your willingness to meet with me today. I have a concern, as a friend and someone who worships with you. We may need to talk about how we can improve our interpersonal communication. I sense that we are becoming distant from each other. Do you think so too?"

At this moment you may hear...silence. Do not fill the space. Do not say, "Well, the last thing I want to do is offend you." There is nothing to apologize for at this moment. Allow for the silence and listen for the response.

If the response is, "I have no idea what you are talking about," be prepared to cite specific instances between the two of you.

Next, use silence to communicate. Let's assume your invitation was accepted when you said, "I sense we have become distant with each other. Do you share my observation?"

When the other person begins to glue words together in response to your question, your response should be a thoughtful silence. Sometimes we communicate how uncomfortable we are by running at the mouth. Actively listening is your best chance of putting this person at ease. The two of you are working at cleaning up the unfounded assumptions that have hobbled your earlier understanding. Silence is the ultimate gift you can give each other.

When you have listened, move into the fourth stage: assertive reflection.

You and I have three choices when the other person has stopped talking. We can be aggressive (moving forward in our chair, raising our voice and issuing threats), or passive (continuing to nod our head and forcing a smile to indicate agreement, but internally vowing we will never give this person the pleasure of intimidating us again), or we can be assertive.

WHEN I DISCOVERED HOW TO BE AN ASSERTIVE SERVANT, I UNCOVERED THE SPIRITUAL AND EMOTIONAL HEALTH THAT RESULTS FROM ACTING OUT THE LIFE OF A COMMITTED CHRISTIAN.

The assertive adult is someone who has the right to express what he/she is thinking and feeling—without apology. Years ago, I wrote a book entitled, *Your Perfect Right*. I wrote it because I was brought up to be passive. I was raised to be polite and agreeable, concluding conversations with, "Do not hesitate to call me if you have further questions," after which I prayed fervently that I would never hear from this person ever again.

When I discovered the honesty and clarity of my choice to be assertive, I no longer had to apologize for sharing what I was thinking and feeling. As a disciple of Jesus Christ I admit I quietly struggle with making promises I have no intention of fulfilling. Choosing to be aggressive or passive are both easy choices. When I was a child I excelled in being passive. If I could look and sound pathetic, I could manipulate people and their emotions all day long. When I discovered how to be an assertive servant, I uncovered the spiritual and emotional health that results from acting out the life of a committed Christian.

The juxtaposition of these simple two words: assertive servant means I can assert myself, or speak without the need to apologize for my thoughts, feelings and opinions, without surrendering my commitment to also be a servant of the Lord Jesus Christ.

In reality, this means that when I talk with another Christian, we do not have to agree on everything. Doctrinal and lifestyle differences are okay. I can reply with respect, saying, "I have a different opinion on this issue. May I explain the process on how I came to this conclusion so we can better understand each other?"

There are two important components to this sentence. First, note I did not say, "I disagree..." Although it is okay to disagree, using the word disagree is confrontational and negative, especially in this instance. Instead of a negative message, I provided an assertive declaration. Most people will not be offended about a different opinion, but most of us would become defensive if we heard the confrontational response, "I disagree."

The next nonconfrontational component of my assertive response was a rational request. When using "I would like to...." or "Here are three advantages of my counterproposal....," you will put the other person at ease. If someone gets uncomfortably close to your face and says, "This will be done my way," the war drums start to rumble in the background. This kind of conversation will be difficult, intimidating, and probably non-productive, while the first one has hope for real understanding.

The fifth assertive skill is to conclude the conversation with, "I sense both of us want more time to work on improving our interpersonal communications. Do you agree?" Remember, human relationships can become distant, broken, and eventually estranged if too much time filled with silence goes by.

An unknown author wrote, "Relationships never die a natural death, they are murdered by ego, attitude and ignorance."

We do not tell other people the truth because the truth often requires us to face the person we know best. Self-examination is not always pleasant and painless. The hard work of speaking the truth to the person in the mirror cannot be minimized. I know all the weaknesses of my business clients, my family, and the other spiritual leaders in my church, and the people who represent me in Washington, D.C. But I am slow and timid about looking at, talking to, analyzing, and correcting the person in my mirror.

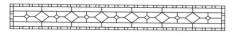

"RELATIONSHIPS NEVER DIE A NATURAL DEATH, THEY ARE MURDERED BY EGO, ATTITUDE AND IGNORANCE."

One of the reasons we do not tell other people the truth about our relationship with each other is because the truth will cost us. We do not get a break from the person in our mirror. Regardless of the date on the calendar, the weather, the political party dominating the White House, our present bank balance, and a million other factors, we have often delayed and avoided a face-to-face with our selves.

This is a book for people of faith. Our faith has been significantly influenced by paging through God's Word. To this day, these sixty-six ancient books continue to drip with the tears of Adam and Eve who chose not to keep a promise, the poor anger management of Moses, David's I-never-get-enough-lust, the petulance of Peter and the thorn in the side of the apostle Paul.

People of faith have, and will continue to, fail. Scripture is precise about the reality of this happening. Paul wrote, *"For I do not understand my own actions. For I do not do what I want, but I do the very thing I hate"* (Rom. 7:15, ESV).

The apostle's words drag us back to the importance of honesty. We have all struggled with the good and the evil we see in ourselves. We celebrate the fact that we have been made in the image of God and He knows our name and walks with us through the labyrinth of our days. And God also knows the truth about us, even though we believe we have fooled everyone else.

We often do not like what we see when we scan the selfishness of our lives. We have often said "I'm too busy" when God is calling us to sit quietly with Him. And the truth is we do not want to hear about the truth again.

CHAPTER TEN

WE DO NOT TELL THE TRUTH TO OTHER CHRISTIANS BECAUSE THE TRUTH WOULD REQUIRE THE CHURCH TO CHANGE

FOR THE PAST thirty years, in addition to my pastoral responsibilities, I have shared my public presentations and organizational skills with corporate America. The client list has included John Deere, Harley Davidson, the U.S. Navy, Texas Instruments, Toyota, and AT&T.

When I moved behind the lectern with my PowerPoint control tightly in my hand, I often wondered, "I wish the church could run its true business (building the kingdom of God) with the same entrepreneurial insight, commitment and expertise as the people seated in front of me." At the end of my work day as an organizational consultant and coach, staring out the window of a taxi on my way to an airport, I often thought about it further, "Why does the church tolerate second best efforts and a limited vision which often cannot see past last Sunday's attendance numbers and offering totals?"

One of the significant books I read during this time was *In Search of Excellence* by Thomas J. Peters and Robert H. Waterman.[43] The authors presented strategies such as goal-setting, brainstorming, valuing your assets, creative problem solving, and aggressive conflict resolution interventions. They also explained the personal perseverance of hungry entrepreneurs. They reminded me no organization can grow and succeed without taking significant risks because the last great idea to produce profitability and growth is still out there.

Unfortunately, much of what the church has created for today is what we have seen, and tried, in our yesterdays. We just keep repeating what will probably not work and then say to each other, "I don't know why our church continues to be present but not powerful."

I have repeatedly heard this statement in conversations with pastoral leadership: "We pay our bills, keep the sanctuary clean, teach our children the tenets of faith…but our congregation continues to limp along and, if the truth be told, we are not growing." These are difficult words for any congregation to hear.

If you, the reader, are convinced our Lord, Jesus Christ called the church to grow and offer healing to a broken world, living mediocre Christian lives is not acceptable. If we have heard the good news, the church should be a gushing spiritual fountain of hope for a world wobbling into destruction. The church has the potential to be the most positive, progressive and healing piece of square footage in an increasingly negative and victimizing world.

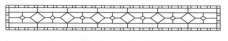

LIVING MEDIOCRE CHRISTIAN LIVES IS NOT ACCEPTABLE.

---

[43] Thomas J. Peters and Robert H. Waterman, *In Search of Excellence: Lessons from America's Best-Run Companies* (London: Profile Books, 2015).

What needs to change in the church? Does the church have the honesty and strength to change? Can we abandon our past practices and the assumptions which have proved to be ineffective when building the kingdom of God and tackle a better plan?

Here are ten areas of the life and mission of the church which need to be reevaluated.

First, the church has to decide if the "us four and no more" mindset is a legitimate excuse for such small growth. Dr. C. Peter Wagner, one of my professors at Fuller Theological Seminary wrote a startling comment about why some churches grow and others decline in his book, *Your Spiritual Gifts Can Help Your Church Grow.*[44] He wrote, "Rare is the church today that will advocate that the professional pastor or staff should do all the ministry of the church."

The "us four and no more" mentality in which only the staff does all the work in a church has never been owned by clergy. The career of the professional clergy person is made secure when he or she can motivate the congregation to bring others to the church. When someone visits a church, the person in the pulpit may wonder if this religious seeker will come back a second time or not, but the grace of God through Christ is most easily detected in the person next to you in the pew. Think about it. The clergy are employed, but the guy sitting next to you is there because he wants to be. The one sharing a hymnal with you or greeting you at the door will be the one that will show whether this religious experience is genuine and reflects Someone larger than those in the sanctuary.

If you are worshipping in a church in which the unstated message among the saints is "us four and no more," it is time to face the facts in light of Scripture. Does Jesus want us to live in tiny prejudiced groups? Is

---

[44] C. Peter Wagner, *Your Spiritual Gifts Can Help Your Church Grow* (Glendale, CA: Gospel Literature, 1979).

this why the church is not numerically growing? If we really have a firm foundation of faith in Jesus Christ, where is our fruit of that? If we are living lives of purpose and peace, why are these pews empty?

Ultimately church growth is not about numbers. Growth in the body of Christ takes place when no one is counting heads. Fortunately, we are the people of the promise and have stumbled into the Holy of Holies where we learned to repeat these words: *"The steadfast love of the Lord never ceases; his mercies ...are new every morning; great is your faithfulness"* (Lam. 3:22-23, ESV).

Whether you are presently engaged in planting a new church or continue to be committed to an already established one, the guarantees of Lamentations 3:22-23 are valid. Yes, God builds His church. But we are accountable to be His voice, presence and power. We should be attracting others. Our lives should naturally draw needy people to the Lord.

We need to ask the question: "Do people who are looking for God, find Him and His unlimited love in us?"

When the choir has sung, the sermon has been preached, the worship bulletin printed without spelling errors, and the benediction pronounced, did the body of Christ grow in wisdom and numbers? If a congregation is in decline, a drop in attendance numbers will be the first alarm to blare the bad news, but the numbers are not the message. The real meaning behind the empty pews is often empty faith.

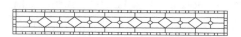

THE REAL MEANING BEHIND THE EMPTY PEWS IS OFTEN EMPTY FAITH.

Christ was explicit about what it means to possess faith. When Peter confessed, *"...'You are the Messiah, the Son of the living God.' Jesus replied, 'Blessed are you, Simon son of Jonah, for this was not revealed to you by flesh and blood, but by my Father in heaven'"* (Matt. 16:16-17).

Again, the church does not grow by numbers. The church grows through humbled, ordinary people who have chosen to step into the blinding presence of God and then begin to hear the beat of a different drummer. And that drumbeat announces our eternity.

If the church is not growing, the people of God need to look at each other and ask, "Why are we not telling each other the truth? Our attendance is down. That is cause for concern. Do people we meet and spend time with know we are even disciples of Jesus Christ? What kind of lives are we living?"

Yes, sometimes the church restrooms could be cleaner, the worship bulletin might have typos, the choir should have spent more time preparing for worship, and the Christmas tree in the sanctuary has seen its better days, but this to-do-list can be easily corrected and fixed. Ultimately what fills the pews is the joyous sounds of people who have been saved by grace. "Us four and no more" is the liturgy of a dying congregation.

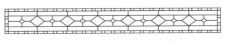

ULTIMATELY WHAT FILLS THE PEWS IS THE JOYOUS SOUNDS OF PEOPLE WHO HAVE BEEN SAVED BY GRACE.

Second, we need to tell each other the truth about clergy-centered worship. Biblical worship was never about the person behind the pulpit.

"Splendor and majesty are before him; strength and joy is in his dwelling place. Ascribe to the Lord, all you families of nations, ascribe to the Lord glory and strength. Ascribe to the Lord the glory due his name; bring an offering and come before him. Worship the Lord in the splendor of his holiness" (1 Chron. 16:27-29).

The responsibility of the church leadership is not to perform but lead a congregation past himself or herself in offering worship to the King of Kings and Lord of Lords.

Church growth in the United States and around the world has exploded in the past decade. In the book, *Witness Essentials,* Dan Meyer provided these statistics: In 1900 Korea had no Protestant church. Today there are over 7,000 Protestant churches in the city of Seoul, South Korea alone. In India, 14 million of the 140 million members of the "untouchable" caste have become Christians.[45]

The people of God, obviously, are the public mouthpiece for the planting and nurturing of the church. At the same time, spiritual leadership is not the bedrock of the church.

Our pastors are shepherds for the body of Christ, not parents.

The history of the church has been filled with names such as Oral Roberts, Kathryn Kuhlman, Chuck Swindoll, Victoria Osteen and John Maxwell. And all of these spiritual leaders have shown us their... feet of clay.

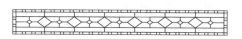

AN HONEST CONVERSATION IN THE BODY OF CHRIST SHOULD REVERE, HONOR, AND AFFIRM OUR SPIRITUAL LEADERS.

An honest conversation in the body of Christ should revere, honor, and affirm our spiritual leaders. We must always be ready, at the same time, to tell the truth. Our faith is built on our relationship with Jesus. He is our Shepherd. It is on Him that we must rely.

Third, within the church we need to have an honest conversation with each other about spiritual boredom and disillusionment. As mentioned before in the Beatles hit, "Eleanor Rigby" there is a reference to a

---

[45] Daniel Meyer, *Witness Essentials: Evangelism That Makes Disciples* (Downers Grove, IL: IVP Connect, 2012).

clergyman, Father McKenzie, who is "writing the words of a sermon that no one will hear. No one comes near. Look at him working, darning his socks in the night when there's nobody there. What does he care?"[46]

The image of Father McKenzie captures the burned-out pastor. At one time, he was spiritually energized in the pulpit, a fool for staring at another sunset, but now he has lived long enough to nod off while serving the Lord's Supper.

Within in the church we also sometimes confront dinosaur disciples of Christ who have lost, with time, their connection with the Almighty. They can give you chapter and verse, all without grace. They have become nominal believers who long ago lost their first love for Christ and His church.

I am suggesting we, who still tear up when singing, "Amazing Grace" consider them in light of the words that follow: "...how sweet the sound that saved a wretch like me. I once was lost but now I'm found, was blind but now I see."[47] We should invite the burned out, and sometimes burned over, Christian to share a cup of coffee and ask this question: "You have been a Christian for many years. What circumstances in your life have challenged your faith? Do you continue to be committed to Christ as the Lord of your life?"

Be prepared. You just asked two assertive questions. Even though you were positive, you may hear a response which centers only on what is wrong in the body of Christ.

Don't debate. Just keep asking questions. Listen carefully to the responses and glue together new questions. This questioning approach will give the person the opportunity to hear himself or herself. That will be good for them and allow the Lord to speak to them.

---

[46] Lennon and McCartney, writers, Eleanor Rigby; Yellow submarine, Parlophone, 1966, CD.

[47] John Newton, writer, "Amazing Grace," 1779, public domain.

You can summarize with a statement like, "If I understood you clearly, you stated ...." When you can accurately reflect what the other person is feeling and thinking, you become an asset to them. Whether you realize it or not, they desperately need you to be that. When you click off all the reasons this person is wrong about his or her assumptions and memories, you become an enemy. But when you listen and care, you become a help.

The truth is that many Christians slide into their final days drenched in anger, resentment, and loneliness because no one in the covenant community of faith has ever asked them to page through their memories about the church, their salvation, and eternity. These conversations will remind them of why they are here and encourage their faith.

Here is someone, at the end of life, who will tell you the truth. Do not argue. Just listen and show forth the acceptance and care our Lord gave us on the cross when He, in pain, forgave the criminal next to Him. Forgiveness and grace are powerful.

Fourth, we have to be honest enough to end our worship wars. Some of us like to be handed a printed liturgy, hymnal, and offering plate. Others like a mammoth screen with the fast-moving words of a worship song accompanied by a six-piece band accented by a very competent drummer. Still others want all that plus the mother of all religious Internet euphoria: live streaming of another worshipping congregation in Brussels, Belgium, or some such place.

Some of us want an expository preacher who will take the Word apart verse by verse. They want to hear a sermon that cites the Hebrew and Greek words and explains the original intent of the biblical author. Other parishioners long for a preacher who can make you laugh at God, yourself, and those seated around you. Still others want to hear stories laced with the Word.

Of all the issues that divide the church, style and content seem to be the most divisive.

There are three reasons why we have such difficulty finding common ground when we are called to worship.

First, we learned a particular style of worship as we grew up, for better or worse. If you grew up with a printed liturgy in your hand and took comfort from knowing when the service began and when it would end, you are looking for a dependable structure in a worship environment. If, on the other hand, you were spiritually nurtured in an atmosphere of spontaneous worship, you are probably looking for a body of believers who are comfortable with new expressions of praise, repentance, and faith.

The second reason we often struggle with sharing our adoration of God with other believers is that we are not sure if we're all on the same page theologically. How do we know that another believer will not attack our understanding of God and the components of our worship? Are we truly safe?

In Nathaniel Hawthorne's novel, *The Scarlet Letter,* Hester Prynne is the chief protagonist in this agonizing story set in the 1600s. Hester failed the spiritual Puritan smell test because she decided to willfully participate in fornication with the Reverend Arthur Dimmesdale, the clergyman

THERE ARE HOLY HOOPS WE HAVE TO JUMP THROUGH TO BE COMFORTABLE IN WORSHIP.

who led her Boston congregation, and to whom she had gone to for help. The scorn from her religious neighbors was deafening. Grace was in short supply. At the end of her life, the letter "A" was placed on her tombstone. Hester Prynne is a fictional character, but she does provide a practical literary illustration of what separates us from each other when we bend our knees together in worship.

There are holy hoops we have to jump through to be comfortable in worship. We want to cluster together with other people who want to do things the same way we do. We want to sing from a hymnal and not read the lyrics from a screen, or vice versa. Some of us look for fellow congregants who partake of the Lord's Supper weekly by physically breaking bread with one another. Others will encourage the preacher in the middle of a sermon with an audible "Amen" or "Hallelujah." We drag our worship history into a new sanctuary and decide if there is a match or not. If the elements of worship overlay our memories, we often feel like we have spiritually come home.

We can also detect dissonance in any act of worship when ancient Scripture challenges our contemporary lifestyles and choices. Some of us were spiritually admonished with these words, "Don't dance, chew, or go with boys (or girls) who do." The clarity of this saying is without question. The words may make you smile because of their simplicity, but, especially in my home as a child, the spiritual and parental implications of

SHELDON BELIEVED THE MARK OF A GENUINE FOLLOWER OF JESUS CHRIST WAS SOMEONE WHO WOULD IMITATE THE LIFE AND MISSION OF CHRIST.

not listening to this could be dire. There is a larger question here: "Does our faith actually impact how we spend our time, talents, and treasure?"

It is far too simple for us, as committed followers of Jesus Christ, to spend our time screaming at each other about lifestyle choices. A redeeming use of turning off the blaring noise in our sanctuaries would be to scan the structure of our spirituality by asking the ultimate question, "What would Jesus do?"

In 1896, Charles Sheldon, a pastor of a Congregational Church in Topeka, Kansas, wrote a book entitled, *In His Steps.* As a result of reading the four Gospels, Sheldon believed the mark of a genuine follower of Jesus Christ was someone who would imitate the life and mission of Christ.

In Sheldon's book he recounts the words of an alcoholic who walked by a church service and heard these lyrics sung by this small congregation:

"All for Jesus, all for Jesus,

All my being's ransomed powers,

All my thoughts, and all my doings,

All my days, and all my hours."[48]

Sheldon concluded the mission of the church could be consolidated into this simple question: "What would Jesus do?" Walking according to our faith as we answer this question in every aspect of our lives will bring us into the center of Jesus' will.

There is no need for the church to immerse itself in once-a-week routine of faith, living hypocritical lives in which we are not honest or happy. The simplicity of this statement is quite staggering: Review the life of Christ and mirror His love, hope, and words to a world that cascades from one crisis to another.

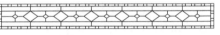

REVIEW THE LIFE OF CHRIST AND MIRROR HIS LOVE, HOPE, AND WORDS TO A WORLD THAT CASCADES FROM ONE CRISIS TO ANOTHER.

We will end our worship wars when the church consistently and continuously asks the question, "What would Jesus do?" And then answers it by acting accordingly. It cuts to the heart of living for Jesus.

The fifth, and final, strategy the church needs to pursue is in reminding one another of our submission to our heavenly Father. He is *our* Father,

---

[48] Charles M. Sheldon, *In His Steps*, Gutenberg.org, August 11, 2009, accessed November 8, 2017, http://www.gutenberg.org/ebooks/4540, 13.

and we must learn to agree with the prayer of Jesus when He said, *"...nevertheless, not as I will, but as you will"* (Matt. 26:39b, ESV).

God has always been dependably realistic with us. Our faith is not wrapped in Elizabethan English with all the appropriate "Thous" and "Thees" littering our spiritual landscape. No. Our faith gets mired in our humanity and our failures.

The good news is God has decided to bury our tendency for religiosity within the simplicity of the Ten Commandments, the practical urgings of the Sermon on the Mount and the wonder of eternity that awaits us as described by John the Revelator.

God has never waited for us to feel religious. God called us to a spiritual life which is constantly evolving, as He brings us deeper into our faith through knowing Him. Our spiritual responsibility is to keep pace with the Lion of the Tribe of Judah who leaps into the future with quiet

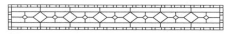

GOD CALLED US TO A SPIRITUAL LIFE WHICH IS CONSTANTLY EVOLVING, AS HE BRINGS US DEEPER INTO OUR FAITH THROUGH KNOWING HIM.

power and mind-numbing grace.

We are called to tell the truth, His truth, to those next to us in the pew and those, not seated in a pew, who are desperately looking for the good news. So be it.

IF YOU'RE A FAN OF THIS BOOK, WILL YOU HELP ME SPREAD THE WORD?

There are several ways you can help me get the word out about the message of this book...

- Post a 5-Star review on Amazon, Goodreads and other places that come to mind.
- Write about the book on your Facebook, Twitter, Instagram, Google+, any social media sites you regularly use.
- If you blog, consider referencing the book, or publishing an excerpt from the book with a link back to my website.
- Take a photo of yourself with your copy of the book. Post it on your social media – email me a copy as well!
- Recommend the book to friends – word of mouth is still the more effective form of advertising.
- When you're in a bookstore, ask them if they carry the book. The book is available through all major distributors, so any bookstore that does not have it in stock can easily order it.
- Do you know a journalist or media personality who might be willing to interview me or write an article based on the book? If you will email mail me your contact, I will gladly follow up.
- Purchase additional copies to give away as gifts.

SPEAKING SCHEDULE...

If you are part of an organization who has guest speakers or you know of an organization who might be interested in having me speak, lead a workshop or make a presentation, please contact me at: callemon@aol.com.